Hosting Cask Ale Events
Practical Advice for Preparing and Serving Real Ale for the Publican, Homebrewer, and Cask Ale Enthusiast

Hosting Cask Ale Events
Practical Advice for Preparing and Serving Real Ale for the Publican, Homebrewer, and Cask Ale Enthusiast

by
Randy Baril

Photographs by Randy Baril, Lia Olberg, or Brittany Burke
Cover Layout by Joanne Powell & Randy Baril
Printing by The Book Patch, www.thebookpatch.com

Copyright © 2016 by Randy Baril
Limited Edition Release NHC '15 Edition: May 2015
First Edition Release: October 2016
Printed in the United States of America
ISBN-10: 1682738531
ISBN-13: 9781682738535

To My Unceasingly Patient Wife Kate,
Ever Indulgent and Forgiving

Table of Contents

Acknowledgement

There are many without whom this book would have been impossible. First and foremost are the members of the NERAX Working Party, those tireless volunteers who make the New England Real Ale eXhbition happen festival after festival through dedication and perseverance. Without your work there would have been no cellar for me to learn in. To name but a few names: John Sheridan, who suggested I volunteer in the first place, Dave Wilson and Mike Labbe, cellarmen before me, and Mark Bowers, festival organizer these past years.

This book would never have existed had it not been for John Sullivan, Eamon Poplin, Max Heinegg, and Tony Corsentino. Not every self-published book gets to come into being under the watchful eye of a professional publisher, an award-winning journalist, a high school English teacher, and a master of the library arts! Homebrewers all; this hobby does attract all sorts.

And the Boston Wort Processors, who indulged me in 2013 when I suggested that our club night appearance at the National Homebrewer's Conference in Philadelphia should be an all-cask presentation "just like a miniature NERAX." To the finest group of homebrewers I've had the opportunity to freely associate with, I say "Cheers!"

Randy Baril

C H A P T E R   O N E

Why Cask Ale?

In a word, flavor. Cask ale has flavors that standard keg beer lacks because it is served at a different temperature, lower carbonation, and is continually worked by living yeast interacting with the changing conditions inside the service vessel (usually a cask). When done right, there is nothing as satisfying as a pint of *proper*[1] pulled with practiced care. This experience has inspired such fervent devotion that in the United Kingdom there is a *Campaign for Real Ale (CAMRA)* that is fanatical in the defense of this ideal.

"Brewed as cold as the Rockies" is a familiar tag line for a representative American macro-lager. While undeniably refreshing and incredibly technical to make, this style of beer is served cold so that your taste buds are numbed to the point where they do a poor job[2] recognizing the flavor of the beverage being consumed. This is to disguise the fact that the beverage itself doesn't actually have much flavor. Brewing to exacting standards with a minimum of cost-effective ingredients is bound to have an impact on flavor and, if the emphasis is shifted to refreshment via strong marketing campaign, that flavor can take a back seat.

---

[1] Terms appearing with this emphasis are found further defined in the glossary.

[2] "Temperature of served water can modulate sensory perception and acceptance of food," Food Quality and Preference, Volume 28, Issue 2, June 2013, Pages 449–455

At warmer temperatures taste receptors are better able to discern flavors that would be lost in the same beverage served at frosty temperatures. Malt flavors come to the fore as aromatic compounds are released. A perception of the thickness or *gravity* of the beer begins to fill the mouth, giving the beer a fuller "mouthfeel." This continues as temperature rises until the beer begins to lose that refreshing quality. A beer too close to room temperature isn't very refreshing. Too cold and it isn't very flavorful. The happy medium is called *cellar temperature*, which is 48 – 54°F.

"Cellar temperature" is a storied term. Legend would have you believe that it is the consistent temperature of a dug earthen cellar, about six to ten feet below grade. The practical reality of it was that refrigeration as we know it today did not exist before 1834. It did not become commonplace until much later, perhaps as late as the first World War. Subterranean storage, where it did exist, made for a good place to store the local brewery's wares. The temperature in a cellar is more consistent and cooler than the above-ground area. A consistent cooler temperature is better for perishable goods such as beer.

The way cask ale is prepared for service also has an effect on flavor. The most obvious perceivable difference is the lower *carbonation* levels of cask ale. It is less fizzy. This is apparent in both smell and taste. In the nostril, there is significantly less of a burning sensation due to gaseous CO_2 converting to carbonic acid on your mucal membranes. This same acid is also reduced in solution so the beer has a bit less "bite" than the same beer with a standard level of carbonation. The reduced carbonation also has some subtle impacts on the way the chemistry of flavors in the beer evolves while it is packaged.

Less fizz means that the beer doesn't smell as strongly. Those aromatic compounds are still there (and more abundant, given the warmer temperature as discussed above), but they are no longer being lifted off the beer by the escaping CO_2. They stay closer to the surface of the beer and contribute to a richer beer flavor as they are best appreciated as the beer is being consumed.

The traditional service method for cask ale is to breach the vessel above the beer and allow air in to replace the volume of beer dispensed. This exposure to air introduces not only potential *spoilage organisms* but also atmospheric oxygen. The latter of these is typically more relevant as any spoilage organisms introduced lack the time to detrimentally effect the flavor. Usually a contaminated beer can be traced back to bacterial loading at the brewery.

Oxygen is a highly reactive gas that participates in many chemical reactions. It can have a staling effect on beer flavor (wet cardboard) and a mellowing effect on harsh alcohols. The geometry of the vessel with its single small port at the top and the relatively undisturbed interior airspace above a beer slowly off-gassing CO_2 causes these reactions to happen slowly. It is terrifically informative to try the same beer over several days of service to fully appreciate the effect oxidation has on a maturing beer. The flavor changes over time!

Cask ale is an option for beer service. Some beers are simply better on draught or in bottles. Two examples are Imperial IPAs (the higher concentration of hop aromatics are readily lifted by the higher carbonation levels) and lambics (the thinner body helps compensate for the far greater acidity of the style). This is not a polemic to convince you that cask ale is the only way to enjoy your beer. The fact that the styles that do best on cask happen to be the more interesting styles to consume is an exercise left to the reader.

Defining Cask Ale

Let's differentiate between cask ale and real ale. *Real ale* is any beer (ale or lager, despite the name) that has undergone a secondary fermentation in a sealed vessel. Because the vessel is sealed, the carbon dioxide (CO_2) produced by the yeast, and only the yeast, is trapped and has nowhere to go but into solution. This carbonates the beer, giving it *condition*. The terms "carbonation" and "condition" will be used interchangeably in this text.

There are a variety of vessels that real ale can be conditioned in. Since the late 1500s, bottles have been the vessel of choice for highly carbonated beer. That's right – homebrewed beer is real ale when it is bottle conditioned! Before that, wooden casks or ceramic crocks were used. The structural integrity of these vessels was a limiting factor in how much condition a beer could develop. Too much and they would burst! As you can read in the sidebar, there has long been debate about the role of carbonation in beer. So long as the yeast is the only source of CO_2, you are making real ale.

"It is a great custom and general fashion nowadays to bottle ale; but the same was never invented by any true naturalist that understood the inside of things. For though ale be never so well wrought or fermented in the barrel, yet the bottling of it puts it on a new motion or fermentation, which wounds the pure spirits and ... body; therefore such ale out of bottles will drink more cold and brisk, but not so sweet and mild as the same ale out of a cask, that is of a proper age: besides the bottle tinges or gives it a cold hard quality, which is the nature of glass and stone, and being the quantity is so small, the cold Saturnine nature of the bottle has the greater power to tincture the liquor with its quality. Furthermore, all such bottle drinks are infected with a yeasty furious foaming matter which no barrel-ale is guilty of ... for which reason bottle-ale or beer is not so good or wholesome as that drawn out of the barrel or hogshead; and the chief thing that can be said for bottle-ale or beer is that it will keep longer than in barrels, which is caused by its being kept, as it were, in continued motion or fermentation."

A New Art of Brewing Beere
circa 1691

Cask ale is real ale served from a vessel with separate ports for gas exchange and liquid to be drawn out. Some common vessels include the English casks for which this style is named, German (Franconian) gravity kegs, the Cornelius-style kegs common in home-brewing, stainless steel 5L mini-kegs, and even standard commercial Sanke kegs.

The one exception I'm familiar with is from David Line's classic *Big Book of Brewing*[3] where UK homebrewers were encouraged to make real ale in a collapsible water container. One could serve perfectly conditioned real ale from such a vessel by orienting the serving spout to be at the top, venting the excess CO_2 at the appropriate time, then gently rotating the container into serving orientation and allowing the container to collapse as pints were pulled. A modern interpretation of this is the KeyKeg or KeyCask, which as of this writing was still finding favor as a non-returnable beer distribution vessel.

This definition of cask ale focuses on yeast-produced CO_2 and does not require service from the vessel in which the secondary fermentation occurred, nor does it require the introduction of atmospheric oxygen. For these reasons, it fails the **CAMRA definition of cask ale**. This is perfectly fine. CAMRA should hold the line and stick with *the* historic definition of cask ale. Our modern times allow for additional strategies to get the benefits of cask ale while avoiding some of the pitfalls in order to get more cask ale *done well* to the drinking public. This allows for such strategies as: all of the German cask ales, *rack-bright beer*, *blanketed service*, and a host of other strategies.

---

[3] Line, David. The *Big Book of Brewing*

CHAPTER TWO

Cask Anatomy and Preparation

A Few Silly Words Associated with Cask Ale

Cask ale is often described in British imperial units, which are slightly different from the American units to which the reader may be accustomed. An imperial gallon is roughly 1.2 American gallons. An imperial barrel is 36 imperial gallons, or 43.23 American gallons. This is notably different from an American brewer's barrel of 31 American gallons. A variety of smaller vessels, such as the *pin*, *firkin*, and *kilderkin*, are used to distribute the prepared cask ale in a volume more reasonable for a *cellarman* to physically handle. There are also a few unreasonable vessels such as the *tun*, *butt*, and *hogshead* typically used by the brewery for special occasions where mass consumption is expected.

Of amusement to the author is that the term "baril" is found in medieval French to be a unit of liquid measure. Since families routinely took names intimately associated with their vocation, a Baril was most likely a winemaker or brewer.

A firkin, from Middle Dutch vierdekijn, meaning "fourth", is a quarter of an imperial barrel, or 9 imperial gallons. While this does convert to 10.8 American gallons of capacity, a firkin usually holds closer to 10.6 gallons of primed beer.

a pin and a firkin

A pin is equal to half a firkin (4.5 imperial gallons or 20 liters). Similarly, while this converts to 5.4 American gallons of capacity, there is usually closer to 5.3 gallons of primed beer. This is just a bit bigger than the Cornelius-style kegs popular in homebrewing.

Pins, firkins, and all vessels that transport beer are collectively called ***cooperage.*** All of these words will be used interchangeably except when a size is specified.

Anatomy of a Cask

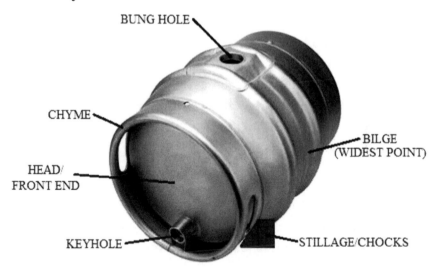

Stillaging a Cask

A ***stillage*** is where the beer is placed while it is prepared for service. For a festival, this could be the table or stand that the beer is placed. A commercial cellar will doubtlessly have a permanent stillage. There are a great number of ways to position the cask for service, such as ***chocking*** the cask, placing it on a stand, using an auto-tilt stillage, or using a more permanent solution. Generally a beer is placed onto the stillage, then vented, tapped, and served.

two examples of stillages

On the left is a custom-built wooden pin cradle and enclosure used at Atwood's in Cambridge, MA. On the right is a temporary stillage built with scaffolding in use at the 2013 NERAX festival. *Cask cradles* are great for holding a single cask for service. When working with a large number of casks, storing many cradles can be impractical. A cheap and easy way to stillage your cask is to use chocks.

A *chock* is a wooden block usually cut from a pine 2x4. The most convenient size is a 3" x 4" X 5" right triangle. Due to the specific dimensions of the wood it ends up being a slightly larger, as seen below. Do not sand, polish, or otherwise finish the wood as a rougher surface provides greater friction for the task at hand.

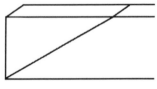

Chocking a cask takes three chocks arrayed in a three-point stance. The front two chocks lift and secure the front against rolling laterally. The rear chock lifts and tilts the vessel during service. The three-point stance is remarkably stable, holding the cask still and allowing for settling to occur.

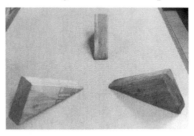

Start with the front two chocks. Always orient the chock so that the hypotenuse (longest side) is down as this gives the greatest surface area to grip the stillage. If the stillage surface is particularly hard and slippery, such as the Formica pictured, spread a cloth below the cask. The tensile strength of the cloth will keep the chocks from sliding apart. Tip the cask back and orient the front two chocks so that they are perpendicular to the surface of the cask. Different cask manufacturers have slightly different geometries so try to find the angle that the chocks grip the cask with the most contact surface area. Be sure to orient the cask so that the keystone is at 6 o'clock, at the very bottom of the *front end*.

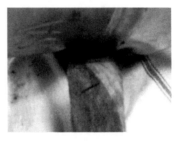

Once the front chocks are securely placed, raise the back of the cask and place the third chock in place. When working alone from the front, reach to the back and hug the cask closely, using leverage to pivot the cask onto the front chocks

without straining your back. Don't try to position the rear chock too far forward as this may interfere with *venting* the cask.

Check that the *bilge* has been raised off of the surface. This reduces the transfer of vibration to the beer within the cask and makes the arrangement more stable. Make slight adjustments to the angle of the chocks to ensure that they have the best grip on both the surface and against the side of the cask.

Tools of the Trade for Sealing a Cask

Woody Bits

Plastic *Keystone*
Fills *keyhole* to seal vessel. Holds *tap* in place. Cheap. Works well enough with stainless cooperage provided the beer is not overprimed. Do not use with plastic cooperage!

Wooden Keystone
Fills keyhole to seal vessel. Holds tap in place. Has the advantage of soaking up beer and expanding to seal most leaks.

Plastic Shive, Single Piece
Fills *bung hole* to seal vessel. Is punctured to vent *headspace*. Holds *spile* (hard or soft). Cheap. Do not use with plastic cooperage!

Plastic Shive, Banded Evolution 'C'
Fills bung hole to seal vessel. Is punctured to vent headspace. Holds spile (hard or soft). Much improved over single piece design. Part of a series produced by Rankin.

Wooden Shive

Fills bung hole to seal vessel. Is punctured to vent headspace. Holds spile (hard or soft). Has the advantage of soaking up beer and expanding to seal most leaks.

Bung

Seals keystone after tap has been removed. The 'B' in TOBI *(see below).*

Useful Hand Tools

Deadblow Hammer

Pounds woody bits and taps into position. Deadblow reduces recoil. Much better than traditional ash mallets.

Ash Mallet

A very traditional motivational device great for whacking in taps.

Large Regular Screwdriver

Always a handy lever to have in one's toolkit. Get one with a thick shaft, at least 12" long.

Shive Extractor

The easy way to remove shives. This is a metal bar machined with a burr that makes extracting shives much easier.

Cleaning Your Cooperage

Casks have a tendency to become quite unsanitary. In the trade, an emptied cask will be *TOBI*'d (tap out, bung in with a spile pounded in to seal the vessel) and left to sit unwashed for weeks if not months before rotating back to the brewery. The living yeast that worked the beer is still very much still alive inside the cask. Most cask service allows air in as the beer is drained, pretty much guaranteeing the introduction of an acetobacter in addition to a potpourri of other spoilage organisms that colonize the empty vessel. Together they produce a unique aroma enjoyed by the unfortunate few who are tasked with cleaning them for refilling. This is a completely different experience than when working with sealed kegs that were emptied under a blanket of CO_2.

Some breweries have specialized cleaning apparatus that use some combination of scalding temperatures, strong *caustic*s, and powerful sprayers to scour the microbial interlopers from the cask. This cleaning and *sanitizing* regime must be harsh. Should any organism survive, the next beer *racked* into the cask will be at great risk of being condemned before service. While this is an accepted reality in the English cask ale trade, American distributors and breweries have had a hard time getting the hang of the rhythm of the cleaning regimen necessary for cask ale.

Homebrewers have a terrific advantage when it comes to reducing spoilage as they maintain complete control over their cooperage. Much like with glass bottle reuse, an ounce of prevention in the form of rinsing immediately after use is worth a pound (or at least a few ounces) of cleanser. Simply rinsing away the remaining contents upon emptying the vessel dramatically reduces available food sources for spoilage organisms. Leaving the vessel open as opposed to sealing it encourages the interior to dry out, further frustrating these organisms. Of course, sanitizing before storage makes for an even more inhospitable environment.

For the breweries that are without specialized equipment (or the lazy homebrewer), cleaning a ripe cask is not particularly onerous once you get past the smell. Simply remove the old woody bits, then rinse with hot water (tap-hot is fine) until it runs out relatively clear. Visually check for and make note of chunks of stuck-on matter as well as you can. We just want to be sure that they come off after the hot soak.

Depending on how you prefer to fill the vessel, sanitize the appropriate orifice and insert either the keystone (for filling via the bung hole) or shive (for filling via the key hole). I prefer to fill via the key hole so that the cask stands on end without chocks. Many breweries and those adding significant dry-hops or other late flavoring agents prefer to fill via the bung hole. It makes no difference.

Fill the vessel with hot water, the hotter the better, up to 180°F. Add a strong cleanser such as Powdered Brewery Wash (PBW) in a strong cleaning solution. Let stand and soak as directed. Drain. Check that those trouble spots are now clean, then rinse with hot water to remove any residue. Use a brush to scrub as necessary.

Thoroughly sanitize the vessel. I prefer to use a one gallon solution of StarSan because I can slosh it around and it will leave sanitizing foam clinging to interior surfaces. Any no-rinse sanitizing solution will also work. I alternate sloshing and resting in various orientations to make sure that the bung area, the back end, the ullage, and the back side of the front end all get some time submerged by the StarSan solution. I have a solid #8½ rubber stopper to temporarily fill the keyhole while soaking the interior of the front end. You can use a solid #11 rubber stopper or a fresh shive gently pressed into position to temporarily seal the bung hole. Once sanitized, drain away the sanitizer and fill immediately with fresh beer. When using StarSan, *do not fear the foam™*.

How to Prime a Cask

Cask ale is best served at 1.1 – 1.3 dissolved *volumes of CO2* (less than half of the usual volume of packaged beer), although it can be found served with as high as 1.75 dissolved volumes of CO_2. Fermented beer has a certain volume of CO_2 present in solution at the end of fermentation. This amount is temperature-dependent (cold beer holds on to more CO_2) and can be found on the chart to the right.

Dissolved Volumes of CO₂ Present after Fermentation

Temperature °F (°C)	Volumes CO_2
47 °F (8.33 °C)	1.21
50 °F (10.0 °C)	1.15
53 °F (11.7 °C)	1.09
56 °F (13.3 °C)	1.04
59 °F (15.0 °C)	0.99
62 °F (16.7 °C)	0.94
65 °F (18.3 °C)	0.89
68 °F (20.0 °C)	0.85
71 °F (21.7 °C)	0.81
74 °F (23.3 °C)	0.77
77 °F (25.0 °C)	0.73
80 °F (26.7 °C)	0.69
83 °F (28.3 °C)	0.66

Table 2.1

We want 1.4 dissolved volumes in our finished, unbreached cask. This assures us of the 1.3 volumes we want while reducing the concern over blowing a shive or keystone. To get there, simply subtract the volumes expected to be in your beer from 1.4.

Example 1: Merkin's Best Bitter has finished its fermentation at 65°F. Using the Table 2.1, we'd expect there to be .89 dissolved volumes of CO_2. Since we want to raise the beer to 1.4 volumes after conditioning, we need to create .51 (1.4 – .89) dissolved volumes of CO_2 in the conditioning vessel.

Priming with Dextrose

Dextrose		Volumes of CO_2 per		
oz	(g)	5 Gallon (19L)	pin	firkin
1	(28)	0.34	0.32	0.16
1.5	(43)	0.51	0.48	0.24
2	(57)	0.68	0.64	0.32
2.5	(71)	0.85	0.80	0.40
3	(85)	1.02	0.96	0.48
3.5	(99)	1.19	1.12	0.56
4	(113)	1.36	1.28	0.64
4.5	(128)	1.53	1.44	0.72
5	(142)	1.70	1.60	0.80
5.5	(156)	1.87	1.76	0.88
6	(170)	2.04	1.92	0.96
6.5	(184)	2.21	2.08	1.04
7	(198)	2.37	2.24	1.12
7.5	(213)	2.54	2.40	1.20
8	(227)	2.71	2.56	1.28
8.5	(241)	2.88	2.72	1.36
9	(255)	3.05	2.88	1.44

Table 2.2

The most common and easiest-to-use priming agent is *dextrose*, a liner form of the monosaccharide glucose. This is also known as corn sugar, dextrose monohydrate, glucose monohydrate, or glucose.h2o. It is the simplest form of glucose and the easiest one for tired yeast to digest. The terms "dextrose", "corn sugar", and "priming sugar" will be used interchangeably. Use Table 2.2 on the previous page to decide how much dextrose you need to create the necessary volumes of CO_2.

Example 1, continued: We are filling a pin with Merkin's Best Bitter. We need to create an additional .51 dissolved volumes of CO_2. Per Table 2.2, we need a little more than 1.5 ounces of dextrose. (.51 is a little more than .48.) Let's use 1.6 oz of dextrose to ensure that we get where we want to go.

Simply boil this amount of dextrose in a small amount of water to sanitize and add it to the vessel as you're filling it. A two-minute boil is sufficient. For a pin, use a cup of water. For a firkin, use two. Some brewers will skip the sanitization step but this is bad practice. Your beer will never be as vulnerable to spoilage organisms as when it is being transferred to the *service vessel*. While certain brewpubs may be able to get away with sloppy practice by quickly turning over the beer, bad practice will never yield consistently great results. I prefer to add my priming agents before *racking* the beer to ensure that they're in there.

Other *fermentables* can also be used as a priming agent, including unfermented *wort* of known specific gravity, as seen in Table 2.3 on the following page.

The selection of your priming agent can impact the flavor of the finished beer. As John Palmer put it, "Do you want to keep the priming sugar hiding in the wings or do you want to bring it onstage?"[4] It is left to the brewer to decide if this is desirable.

Using the weight of dextrose calculated above, we can determine the weight of any fermentable listed on this chart necessary to sufficiently carbonate the beer by using the following formula[5]:

(Weight of A)(Percent Solids of A)(Fermentability of A)
= (Weight of B)(Percent Solids of B)(Fermentability of B)

Since we're standardizing our calculation using dextrose, the left side of the equation becomes:

(Weight of A)(95%)(100%) =
(Weight of B)(Percent Solids of B)(Fermentability of B)

Once an alternate priming agent has been selected, the data for Percent Solids and Fermentability come from the chart.

> **Example, continued 1:** Merkin's Best Bitter relies on a hint of maple to give it the characteristic sweet finish. We calculate the amount of maple syrup necessary to carbonate by filling in the formula and solving.

$$(1.6 \text{ oz})(95\%)(100\%) = X (66\%)(100\%)$$
$$1.52 \text{ oz} = X (66\%)$$
$$2.3 \text{ oz} = X$$

> Therefore we require 2.3 oz (65 g) of Maple Syrup to gain the .51 dissolved volumes of CO_2 necessary to sufficiently carbonate the beer in our pin.

---

[4] Palmer, *How to Brew*, 110-111

Alternate Fermentables for Priming[5]

Fermentable	Extract Yield (PPG*)	% Ferment- ability	Constituents
Dextrose (Corn Sugar)	42	100%	Glucose (~5% moisture as dextrose monohydrate, 0% moisture as anhydrous dextrose)
Belgian Candi Sugar	46	100%	Sucrose, inverted
Honey	38	95%	Fructose, Glucose, Sucrose (~18% water)
Lactose	46	0%	Lactose (<1% moisture)
Lyle's Golden Syrup	46	100%	Glucose, Fructose (18% water)
Maltodextrine	42	0%	Dextrines (5% moisture)
Maple Syrup	31	100%	Sucrose, fructose, glucose (~34% water)
Molasses / Treacle	36	Varies, ~60%	Sucrose, invert sugars, dextrines.
Rice Syrup Solids	42	Varies. ~80%	Glucose, maltose, other (~10% moisture)
Table Sugar (Sucrose)	48	100%	Sucrose

Table 2.3

* PPG is Points per Pound per Gallon, meaning that if you add a pound of dextrose to a gallon of pure water at 60°F, perfectly mixed, the resultant measured SG would be 1.042, an increase of 42 gravity "points." Adding that same pound of dextrose to five gallons of water would yield an increase of 42/5 = 8.4 "points," an expected increase of 1.0084 specific gravity.

---

[5] Modified from Palmer, *How to Brew*, 245

Carbonation can be obtained with pretty much any substance that contains sugars and has an FDA food label (or do a Google search for "food nutrition facts and analysis"). It's pretty safe to assume that the dietary sugars listed on such a label will be about as fermentable as table sugar (aka cane sugar or sucrose). Calculate the necessary amount of table sugar in ounces using the conversion formula. Convert to grams (all labels give this information in grams). Calculate how many servings you need to get that amount of table sugar. Multiply the number of servings by the serving size (by weight). Convert back to ounces if necessary. Be sure to consider the impact of that much foodstuff on your beer!

Example 2: Wildman Wheat Beer is being put into a firkin and primed with a sour cherry syrup. It finished fermentation at 72°F. There are about .8 dissolved volumes of CO_2 in solution (per Table 2.1). To get to 1.4 dissolved volumes in a firkin, we'd need 3.75 oz of corn sugar (per Table 2.2, firkin column, .6 volumes necessary). To convert this to table sugar, we solve:

$$(3.75 \text{ oz})(95\%)(100\%) = X (100\%)(100\%)$$
$$3.56 \text{ oz} = 100.92 \text{ grams} = X$$

The sour cherry syrup contains 25g of sugar per 100g serving size. We need just over four serving sizes (404 grams or 14.25 oz) of the sour cherry syrup to carbonate this beer.

Alternative Priming Methods

If you are intimately familiar with your beer and know exactly when it will finish fermenting, you can skip the addition of priming sugars by packaging before the beer reaches *final gravity*

(FG, the *specific gravity* [SG] at the end of fermentation. aka terminal gravity). This can be a bit dicey because if you package too late, your beer never carbonates. If you package too early, you could blow a shive.

Example 3: I want to package Merkin's Best Bitter without additional sugars. What should the SG of the wort be? I know this beer well and it always finishes at 1.008. The beer is currently at 68°F so it has about .85 dissolved volumes in solution. To get to 1.4 dissolved volumes I'll need .55 additional volumes or about 1.75 ounces of dextrose. Dextrose contributes 42 gravity Points per Pound per Gallon (PPG), so in my 5.3 gallon vessel it will contribute 7.92 points per pound per pin, which is .495 points per ounce per pin. I need 1.75 ounces to carbonate, which would add .866 gravity points to the pin. So if I package it at 1.009 sg, it should carbonate fine. To make sure, I'd rather package it at 1.010.

There is another tradition of using partially or unfermented wort to prime the beer. This is also known as *krausening*.

Example 4: Dang! This batch hit terminal gravity before I finished my calculation! Good thing I have another batch coming along right on its heels. I still need the equivalent of 1.75 ounces of corn sugar to carbonate. If I measure the batch coming along at 1.020, this means that there are 12 gravity points remaining of fermentation. Dextrose has 42 PPG so this is the equivalent of 4.57 ounces of dextrose in a gallon of this beer. We only need 1.75 ounces of dextrose so we can get that equivalency out of .383 gallons = 49 ounces, which is about 3½ pints. So I add 3½ pints of the nearly fermented beer to my pin, then add the finished beer to top it up.

The yeast in solution will ferment the sugars over the next several days. Just because all of the sugars are consumed doesn't mean that the beer is ready. I recommend allowing it to mature for another two weeks, just as when bottle conditioning homebrewed or commercial beer.

George Fix provides another, more formal way[6] to calculate the krausen used in Examples 3 & 4 above:

$$\frac{V_p}{V_b} = \frac{SG_b}{SG_p} \cdot \frac{C_v}{2.44 \cdot SG_p \cdot F - C_v}$$

where:

V_p = the volume of priming solution (krausening beer) to be added.

V_b = the volume of beer to be primed (including V_p).

SG_b = specific gravity of beer to be primed.

SG_p = specific gravity of priming solution (krausening beer).

F = fractional fermentability of priming solution.

C_v = CO_2 level in volumes.

---

[6] Fix, George. *Vienna, Märzen, Octoberfest.* p69.

THE ONE-PAGE GUIDE TO PRIMING YOUR CASK

1. It is best to fill the cask with beer racked out of the fermenter once the beer has reached final gravity. Cold-crashing is OK, but use the fermentation temperature for the charts below.

2. Determine how much priming sugar you need using this formula:

$$1.4 \text{ [dissolved (volumes of } CO_2)] - \text{Residual } CO_2 \text{ from Fermentation} = \text{Required Volumes of } CO_2$$

3. Look up Required Volumes for your vessel to determine amount of dextrose required to carbonate.

Fermentation Temperature (°F/°C)	Volumes of CO_2
47 °F (8.33 °C)	1.21
50 °F (10.0 °C)	1.15
53 °F (11.7 °C)	1.09
56 °F (13.3 °C)	1.04
59 °F (15.0 °C)	0.988
62 °F (16.7 °C)	0.940
65 °F (18.3 °C)	0.894
68 °F (20.0 °C)	0.850
71 °F (21.7 °C)	0.807
74 °F (23.3 °C)	0.767
77 °F (25.0 °C)	0.728
80 °F (26.7 °C)	0.691
83 °F (28.3 °C)	0.655

Table 1

Volumes CO_2 in a pin	Volumes CO_2 in a firkin	Dextrose/ Corn Sugar (oz.)
0.32	0.16	1
0.48	0.24	1.5
0.64	0.32	2
0.80	0.40	2.5
0.96	0.48	3
1.12	0.56	3.5
1.28	0.64	4
1.44	0.72	4.5
1.60	0.80	5
1.76	0.88	5.5
1.92	0.96	6
2.08	1.04	6.5
2.24	1.12	7

Table 2

Example: Merkin's Best Bitter has finished its fermentation at 65°F. According to Table 1, it has .894 dissolved volumes of CO_2 in solution. 1.4-.894 = .506 dissolved volumes required. We look this up on Table 2. To fill a pin, this means MBB needs ~1.6 oz of dextrose.

4. Sanitize the required dextrose by boiling for 2 minutes in small amount of water. Add to cask while racking beer.

5. Any fermentable can be used to prime the beer. Calculate the equivalency to the required ounces of dextrose.

CHAPTER THREE

Dry Hopping and Flavoring Casks

One of the advantages of using casks over kegs is that each cask can be customized as it is filled. By far the most popular way to customize the cask is to add hops directly to the vessel in a process known as *dry hopping*. This is particularly popular with the citrus-oriented "designer" hops becoming available now in the mid '10s. One could also add spices such as licorice, cinnamon, or hot peppers. I recall a particular cask put together by "Uncle" Frank Fermino, then of Tullycross Tavern in Connecticut, that used peppercorns in a ryebock to great effect. It is also a great time to ensure that your coffee porter actually tastes of coffee.

As mentioned in the last section, selection of your priming agent influences the final flavor. The inclusion of the sour cherry syrup may seem an odd choice as an example but this would be appropriate for a wheat or Berliner Weisse. As a brewer, this allows you to derive multiple products from the same base beer. As novelty is a driving force in customer purchase selection, creating such a variation may be just the ticket to standing out on a crowded draught list.

In the beginning of 2015, Maryland brewery Heavy Seas started a custom cask program where publicans or bar managers could request specific attributes for the cask that would appear on their bar. While such an innovative program has yet to prove itself a successful model, it is highlighting exactly the approach mentioned above. They have categories for specifying dry hops, spices, oak character, and coffee/tea flavors, all of which are covered below.

Dry Hopping

Be they whole hops or pellets, adding hops to a finished beer at packaging is a terrific way to emphasize the hop character of a beer. Whether freshening up a bitter with a bit of Fuggle or creating a novel variation of your IPA by adding a blend of Citra®, Motueka®, and Summit®, adding additional hops to the cask gives greater hop flavors and aromatics in the glass.

Whole hops (sometimes incorrectly referred to as leaf hops despite the useful part of the hop plant being the flower or cone) are definitely the preferred form to dry hop with. Because they are less processed than pelletized hops, many brewers feel that they yield fresher flavors and aromas. One of the drawbacks is that they soak up quite a bit of beer and occupy volume in the cask. For larger dry-hopping bills, pellets or plugs may be a better choice. One additional benefit of whole hops is that when left loose in the cask, they can settle on the tap and actually serve as a coarse filter for the beer. This is better for a cask kept and served in house as rough handling can degrade this ability and cause problems with *floaty bits* later on.

Plugs (also referred to as T-45 pellets) are no longer common in the trade. They are nice to use as they are slightly more compacted than whole hops making it easier to get them in the cask. Typically they are the more traditional hop varieties such as Kent Golding, Fuggle, or Hallertau. They tend to act like whole hops when added and are best contained by a hop bag.

Pellet hops are terrific. Known as T-90 pellets, they are highly compacted, taking up much less room inside the cask. The down side is that because they have been compacted, they are also quite granular and dissolve into mush. This isn't a problem in a fermenter, but in a cask oriented horizontally this mush tends toward the tap, causing clouding and floaty bits. Finer bits can persist through much of a cask and have caused headaches for many a cellarman.

It bears mentioning that hops have natural antimicrobial properties that inhibit beer spoilage organisms. You need not worry that the hops themselves will contaminate your beer.

Whatever form of hop you use, consider using a hop bag. Use either a coarse muslin bag for whole or plug hops or a finer nylon bag for pellets. Boiling or otherwise sanitizing the bag before use is best practice, but this may not be practical, particularly for pellet hops that are heat-sealed in a seamless nylon pack. Knotting the muslin bag is encouraged. Remember to leave room for the hops to expand as they will absorb beer.

Some breweries will try to suspend the hop bag from the shive using a bit of string or nylon fishing line. The nylon line is preferred as it is much easier to sanitize. This is best done if the shive is manufactured with a tiny hole on the side to tie to. In the name of all things sanitary, *do not pinch the line between the bung hole and the shive*! This only creates a weakness in your seal potentially allowing for failure (if overcarbonated the shive is not gripping the cask as well as it could be), premature gas release (aka underconditioned beer), or as a convenient ladder for spoilage organisms to migrate into your cask. Do not allow this.

What follows is a list of various hops available at the time of publication. *Alpha acidity* range is omitted as dry hops do not

25

contribute significant bitterness. You may be surprised by the inclusion of some hops known as bittering-only, but I was surprised by the pleasant peachiness contributed by a Warrior dry hop I once used. Don't judge a hop by its traditional use! I limit my dry hopping amounts to ½ – 1 ounce per pin if I dry hop at all as I feel that I get sufficient character for my purposes. The amount you use is left as an exercise for the brewer.

An Incomplete List of Hops and their Aromatic Qualities

Varietal	Origin	Perception
007: The Golden Hop™	USA	Complex fruity aromas of orange and apricot mesh with hints of black tea-like character and a pleasant fresh herbal bouquet.[4]
Admiral	UK	Pleasant, resinous hop aroma with hints of citrus (orange) and herbal flavors.[1]
Agnus	Czech Rep.	Strong spicy and herbal notes.[5]
Ahtanum™ (Brand YCR 1 cv.)	USA	Floral, earthy, citrus and grapefruit tones.[1]
Amarillo® (VGXP01)	USA	Floral, tropical, and citrus (lemon, orange and grapefruit) characteristics.[1]
Apollo™	USA	Line, pine, grapefruit, onion.[3]
Aramis	France	Very fine spice and herbal notes with subtle citrus characteristics.[1]
Aurora (nee Super Styrian)	Styria (Austria)	Intense and pleasant displaying floral, pine and hoppy characteristics.[1]
Azacca™	USA	Intense tropical fruit profile, with sustained impressions of apricot and very ripe mango and notes of pears, apples and pine.[4]
Belma™	USA	A very clean hop, with a very orange, slight grapefruit, tropical pineapple, strawberry, and melon aroma.[4]
Bitter Gold	USA	No specific aroma characteristics.[1]
Boadicea	UK	Mild floral and spicy characteristics with slightly grassy overtones.[1]
Bobek (aka Styrian B)	Styria (Austria)	Intense and pleasant with floral, pine and hop overtones.[1]
Bor	Czech Rep.	Hoppy, spicy.[3]
Bramling Cross	UK	Strong spice, blackcurrant, loganberry and lemon characteristics.[1]

An Incomplete List of Hops and their Aromatic Qualities

Varietal	Origin	Perception
Bravo™ (Hopsteiner 0146)	USA	Pleasant fruity and floral aroma characteristics.[1]
Brewer's Gold	USA	Spicy, fruity characteristics, black currant.[1]
	Germany	Black currant, fruit and spice characteristics.[1]
Bullion	USA	Strong and zesty blackcurrant characteristics.[1]
Caliente	USA	A little lemon zest and a hint of pine. Dominated by a very distinct stone fruit aroma. Juicy aromas of fresh peach/nectarine/plum.[4]
Calypso™	USA	Apple, pear, tropical, mint.[3]
Cascade	USA	Medium intense floral, citrus and grapefruit tones.[1]
	New Zealand	Exceptional levels of citrus moving more toward grapefruit. Distinct from US Cascade due to "terriour".[2]
Cashmere	USA	Mild herbal aroma with strong melon, lemon, lime and slightly spicy notes.[1]
Celeia (aka Styrian C)	Styria (Austria)	Pleasant and hoppy, similar to traditional European varieties.[1]
Centennial	USA	Medium intensity floral and citrus (lemon) tones.[1]
Challenger (Wye Challenger)	UK	Cedar, green tea and sweet floral characteristics (as a late addition, it can provide crisp, fruity flavors).[1]
	New Zealand	Spicy clean citrusy aroma with distinct herbal notes.[2]
Chelan	USA	Mild floral and citrus characteristics.[1]
Chinook	USA	Distinct, medium intensity spice and pine characteristics with subtle notes of grapefruit.[1]
Citra® (Brand YCR 394 cv.)	USA	Strong citrus and tropical tones of grapefruit, melon, lime, gooseberry, passion fruit and lychee.[1]

An Incomplete List of Hops and their Aromatic Qualities

Varietal	Origin	Perception
Cluster	USA	Strong floral and spicy characteristics.[1]
Columbia	USA	Subtle earth and mild fruit tones.[1]
Columbus (aka Tomahawk, Zeus)	USA	Pungent, black pepper, licorice characteristics with subtle citrus overtones.[1]
Comet	USA	A pungent, wild American aroma with citrus (grapefruit) flavors.[1]
Crystal	USA	Mild, spicy and floral.[1]
Delta™	USA	Apricot, ginger, lemon, earthy.[3]
Denali™	USA	Pineapple, pine, citrus[3]
Dr. Rudi (nee Super Alpha)	New Zealand	Fresh citrus peel, pine and lemongrass flavors.[1]
East Kent Golding	UK	Smooth and delicate with floral, lavender, spice, honey, earth, lemon and thyme overtones.[1]
Ekuanot™ (nee Equinox™ HBC 366)	USA	Renamed in 2016. Pronounced aroma profile with citrus, tropical fruit, floral and herbal characteristics of melon, berry, orange peel, lime, papaya, pine and fresh peppers.[1]
El Dorado™	USA	Watermelon, pear, candy, or stone fruit. Often a citrus undertone.[4]
Ella (nee Stella)	Australia	Spicy, hoppy and floral with hints of anise.[1]
Eroica	USA	Forward fruit flavors.[1]
Eureka™	USA	Black currant, dark fruits, strong herbal notes, pine tree[3]
Experimental HBC 291	USA	Typically described as peppery, floral and fruity.[1]
Experimental HBC 342	USA	Mild citrus, tropical fruit and melon notes.[1]
Experimental HBC 431	USA	Peach, berry, tropical fruit, citrus and herbal.[1]
Experimental HBC 472	USA	Floral, wood, coconut and distinct whiskey/bourbon.[1]
Experimental HBC 682	USA	Neutral flavor, pleasant, strong, earthy.[1]

Randy Baril

An Incomplete List of Hops and their Aromatic Qualities

Varietal	Origin	Perception
Experimental Hopsteiner #04190	USA	Green tea, spicy, herbal[3]
Experimental Hopsteiner #07270	USA	Spicy, Resinous, Tangerine[3]
Experimental Hopsteiner #09326	USA	Grapefruit, Tropical Fruit, Citrus[3]
Falconer's Flight®	USA	HopUnion Blend. Strong fruit and citrus characteristics, with layers of spicy and earthy overtones.[1]
Falconer's Flight® 7C's	USA	HopUnion Blend. Distinct tropical, floral, lemon and grapefruit characteristics.[1]
Fantasia®	Germany	Barth-Haas Blend. Cream & caramel in a fruit-forward hop with traditional Noble characteristics.[5]
First Gold	UK	Slightly spicy, but smooth, with tangerine, orange marmalade, magnolia and floral flavors.[1]
Fuggle	USA	Mild wood and fruit characteristics.[1]
Fuggle	UK	Delicate and pleasant mint, grass and floral tones.[1]
Galaxy	Australia	Distinct citrus, peach and passion fruit flavors.[1]
Galena	USA	Spicy, blackcurrant and citrus (grapefruit) tones.[1]
Glacier	USA	Pleasant hop aroma.[1]
Gold	Slovenia	Honey, oregano, basil, nettle and hay.[1]
Golding	USA	Mild and delicate with sweet floral characteristics.[1]
Green Bullet	New Zealand	Subtle spiciness.[1]
Hallertau	USA	Mild and pleasant, yet spicy, with herbal and floral characteristics.[1]
Hallertau Aroma	New Zealand	Mix of floral and slight citrus character.[2]

30

An Incomplete List of Hops and their Aromatic Qualities

Varietal	Origin	Perception
Hallertau Blanc	Germany	Floral and fruity with passion fruit, grapefruit, pineapple, grape and lemongrass overtones.[1]
Hallertau Mittelfruh	Germany	Mild, yet spicy, with floral and citrus tones.[1]
Helga	Australia	Very mild and pleasant with delicate floral and herbal tones.[1]
Herald	UK	Orange, grapefruit.[3]
Herkules	Germany	Spicy, floral and hop notes with hints of pine, black pepper and melon.[1]
Hersbruker	Germany	Mild, herbal and floral characteristics, with fruity overtones.[1]
Horizon	USA	Pleasant and spicy, with floral characteristics.[1]
Hull (Huell) Melon	Germany	Distinct fruit characteristics including honeydew melon and strawberry flavors.[1]
Idaho 7	USA	Pungent tropical fruit and citrus (think apricot, orange, red grapefruit, papaya) with big notes of resiny pine and hints of black tea.[4]
Jarrylo®	USA	Banana, pear, orange and spice.[4]
Kazbek	Czech Rep.	Can show a dominant bright citrus note of lemon or grapefruit, but never obscures the quintessential mixture of floral and earthy spice of its Saaz parent.[4]
Kohatu	New Zealand	Fresh tropical fruit characters and an excellent finish and bitterness.[1]
Lemondrop™	USA	Lemon, mint, green tea, slight melon/mango.[3]
Liberty	USA	Mild and spicy with subtle lemon and citrus characteristics.[1]
Loral™	USA	Very pleasant, floral, peppery, lemon-citrus and dark fruit.[2]
Lublin (Lubelski)	Poland	Mild aroma typical of classic noble hops.[1]

An Incomplete List of Hops and their Aromatic Qualities

Varietal	Origin	Perception
Magnum (Hallertau Magnum)	USA	No distinct aroma characteristics.[1]
	Germany	A delicate aroma with inclinations towards floral and fruit flavorings and a prevalent hoppy tang.[1]
Mandarina Bavaria	Germany	Distinct tangerine and citrus flavors.[1]
Marynka	Poland	Grapefruit, lime, anise.[3]
Medusa™	USA	Intense guava, melon, apricot and citrus fruit.[4]
Melba™	Australia	Passionfruit, Grapefruit, citrus and summery characteristics[3]
Merkur (Hallertau Merkur)	Germany	Strong earthy, floral and citrus impressions.[1]
Millennium	USA	Mild and resinous with floral and herbal tones.[1]
Monroe	Germany	Raspberry notes with orange syrup and a sweet taste that reminds one of summer and cherries.[5]
Mosaic™ (HBC 369 cv)	USA	A complex array of tropical fruit, citrus, berry, herbal, earthy and pine characteristics.[1]
Motueka	New Zealand	Lively lemon and lime tones with background hints of tropical fruit.[1]
Moutere (nee Brooklyn)	New Zealand	Intense fruit, citrus and resinous pine, with notes of baking spice and sweet hay.[2]
Mt. Hood	USA	Mild, herbal and somewhat pungent or spicy.[1]
Mt. Rainier	USA	Excellent floral and noble aromas, with citrus and licorice overtones.[1]
Nelson Sauvin	New Zealand	Distinct cool climate and white wine "fruitiness" with fresh crushed gooseberry and grape flavors.[1]
Newport	USA	Mild.[1]
Northdown	UK	Pleasant spice, cedar and pine characteristics with hints of floral and berry flavors.[1]

An Incomplete List of Hops and their Aromatic Qualities

Varietal	Origin	Perception
Northern Brewer	USA	Medium intensity, pine and mint characteristics.[1]
	Germany	Medium intense herbal and floral tones.[1]
Nugget (Hallertau Nugget)	USA	Mild and pleasant with spicy, herbal tones.[1]
	Germany	Fruity, sugar-like, mint, pineapple.[3]
Olympic	USA	Citrus characteristics with subtle spicy notes.[1]
Opal	Germany	Even dispersal of all aroma characteristics - fruity, floral, herbal and hoppy tones all appear.[1]
Orbit	New Zealand	Blend of "Hops with a Difference" breeding program. Varies annually.[2]
Orion	Germany	Gratifying hoppy noble aroma.[3]
Outeniqua	South Africa	Punchy.[3]
Pacific Gem	New Zealand	No distinct characteristics. Some brewers have noted delicate blackberry and floral or oak tones.[1]
Pacific Jade	New Zealand	Bold herbal aromas with hints of fresh citrus and crushed black pepper.[1]
Pacifica (nee NZ Pacific Hallertau)	New Zealand	Classic Hallertau character with some citrus and floral notes.[1]
Palisade® (Brand YCR 4 cv)	USA	Apricot, grass and clean floral charcteristics.[1]
Perle	USA	Slightly spicy with herbal and floral characteristics.[1]
	Germany	Delicate floral, fruit, spice and mint tones.[1]
Phoenix	UK	Crisp and mellow tones of pine, chocolate, molasses and spice characteristics.[1]
Pilgrim	UK	Distinct fruit and spice character with lemon, grapefruit, pear and berry.[1]
Pilot	UK	Lemon, spice and marmalade flavor.

An Incomplete List of Hops and their Aromatic Qualities

Varietal	Origin	Perception
Pioneer	UK	Distinctly hoppy with pleasant citrus (lemon and grapefruit) tones and hints of herbal, cedar flavors.[1]
Polaris	Germany	Intense floral and pleasant mint tones.[1]
Premiant	Czech Rep.	Pleasant, mild aroma.[1]
Pride of Ringwood	Australia	Pronounced and pleasant, a distinct Australian aroma with cedar, oak and herbal tones.[1]
Progress	UK	Moderately strong spicy, grassy, floral, mint, earth and honey tones.[1]
Rakau	New Zealand	Fresh orchard fruits, specifically apricot with some resinous pine needle characteristics are noted.[1]
Relax	Germany	Cornflower and alpine meadows with lemongrass and hibiscus. Minor hints of honeydew melon.[5]
Riwaka	New Zealand	Delicate citrus and passionfruit.[2]
Saaz	USA	Mild spice and earth tones.[1]
	Czech Rep.	Very mild, with pleasant earthy, herbal and floral overtones.[1]
Santiam	USA	Slightly spicy with herbal and floral characteristics.[1]
Saphir (Sapphire)	Germany	Distinct spicy, fruit and citrus (tangerine) tones.[1]
Select	Germany	Floral and fruit characteristics.[1]
Simcoe® (Brand YCR 14 cv)	USA	Unique passionfruit, pine, earth and citrus characteristics.[1]
Sladek	Czech Rep.	Fruity flavor profile including hints of peach, grapefruit and passion fruit.[1]
Smaragd (Emerald)	Germany	Predominantly fruity with strong floral and hop tones.[1]
Sonnet	USA	Goldings-like with floral notes.[4]
Sorachi Ace	USA	Unique lemon and dill characteristics.[1]

An Incomplete List of Hops and their Aromatic Qualities

Varietal	Origin	Perception
Southern Brewer	South Africa	No outstanding flavor or aroma qualities.[3]
Southern Cross	New Zealand	A delicate balance of citrus and spice, including a heady mix of lemon peel and pine needles.[1]
Southern Promise	South Africa	Grapefruit, ginger, apricot.[3]
Southern Star	South Africa	Grapefruit, pear, rose, orange, gooseberries.[3]
Sovereign	UK	Pleasant but intense fruity flavors with mild floral, grassy, herbal and mint characteristics.[1]
Spalt	Germany	Mild and herbal, with spicy, floral and fruit tones.[1]
Spalter Select	Germany	Earthy, citrusy aroma.[1]
Sterling	USA	Herbal and spicy, with a hint of floral, citrus (lemon/pineapple) characteristics.[1]
Sticklebract	New Zealand	Citrus, pine.[3]
Strisselpalt	France	Very fine spicy, herbal, floral, lemon and other fruit tones.[1]
Styrian (Savinjski) Golding	Styria (Austria)	Very mild, noble hop flavor.[1]
Summer	Australia	Balanced citrus, melon and light apricot tones.[1]
Summit™	USA	Distinct spice, earthy, onion, garlic and citrus (pink grapefruit, orange and tangerine) tones.[1]
Super Galena™	USA	Grass, herbal.[3]
Super Pride	Australia	Mild and pleasant subtle resin and fruit tones.[1]
Sussex	UK	Delicate (similar to Fuggle).[1]
Sylva	Australia	Complex and subtle, floral and herbal characteristics.[1]
Tahoma	USA	Predominate citrus and lemon notes with cedar, pine, floral, pepper and subtle green melon notes.[1]

An Incomplete List of Hops and their Aromatic Qualities

Varietal	Origin	Perception
Taiheke	New Zealand	Resinous with exceptional levels of citrus with tropical fruit.[2]
Target	UK	An intense English hop aroma with distinct spicy, floral, sage and citrus characteristics.[1]
Taurus (Hallertau Taurus)	Germany	Strong noble characteristics.[1]
Tettnang	USA	Noble aroma that is pleasant and spicy.[1]
	Germany	Mild and pleasant with balanced earthy, herbal and floral aroma impressions.[1]
TnT®	Germany	Barth-Haas Blend. Citrus, sweet fruit and green fruit flavors. Tends towards a red berry (pomegranate) and spice character.[5]
Topaz	Australia	Resinous, grassy tones with light tropical flavors.[1]
Tomahawk® (aka Columbus, Zeus)	USA	Pungent, black pepper, licorice, curry and subtle citrus.[1]
Tradition (aka Hallertau Tradition)	Germany	Medium intense floral and herbal (grassy) tones.[1]
TriplePearl	USA	Pleasant and balanced with notes of melon, orange citrus, resin, spice and pepper.[1]
Triskel	France	Strong floral, fruit and citrus characteristics.[1]
Ultra	USA	Mild and pleasant with spicy, floral tones.[1]
Vanguard	USA	Herbal and floral tones.[1]
Vic Secret™	Australia	Pineapple, pine, passionfruit. A lighter version of Galaxy.[3]
Wai-iti	New Zealand	Fresh peaches and apricot characteristics; freshly squeezed limes with top notes of mixed citrus and spice.[1]
Waimea	New Zealand	Intense tangelo and citrus fruit with subtle pine characteristics.[1]

An Incomplete List of Hops and their Aromatic Qualities

Varietal	Origin	Perception
Wakatu	New Zealand	Restrained floral notes and freshly zested lime.[1]
Warrior® (Brand YCR 5 cv)	USA	Mild and resinous with subtle citrus, pine and herbal characteristics.[1]
WGV (Whitbread Golding Variety)	UK	Fresh earthy, botanical and floral flavors.[1]
Willamette	USA	Mild and pleasant, with slightly spicy and floral tones.[1]
Yakima Gold	USA	Mild and pleasant.[1]
Yellow Sub	Germany	Barth-Hass blend. Apricot and orange, with a hint of blackberries.[5]
Zeus (aka Columbus, Tomahawk®)	USA	Black pepper, herbal, garlic, slight citrus.[3]
Zythos®	USA	HopUnion Blend. Emulates Amarillo®. Distinct tropical (pineapple) and citrus tones, with slight pine characteristics.[1]

Information comes from the following websites as posted in February 2015.

1. http://www.hopunion.com/hop-varieties/
2. http://www.nzhops.co.nz
3. http://hopsteiner.com/variety-data-sheets/
4. http://bsghandcraft.com/hops/hop-pellets-domestic.html
5. http://www.barthhaasgroup.com/en/varieties-and-products

For the purposes of this table, "nee" means "originally released as".

For a searchable form of this table please visit:
http://www.maydaycask.com/an-incomplete-list-of-hops-2016/

Adding Spices

At their core, hops are really just another spice added to beer. A delicious and beneficial spice, but still just a spice like any other. Research gruit blends if you're interested in unhopped beers. Any other spice can also be used. Some will undoubtedly taste better than others. Use good judgment and moderation as a guide. Some spices get stronger over time by giving up their flavor slowly. Some degrade rather quickly. Refer to Randy Mosher's *Radical Brewing* for guidance on using various spices (especially Chapter 12: "Hops Are Just Another Spice, Mon"). To get more control over the flavor contribution, consider doing an alcohol or water extraction and adding the resultant extract in measured doses.

I asked Uncle Frank about his thought process leading to that peppercorn ryebock mentioned earlier. He was inspired by a recipe he saw in a book by Sam Cagalione[7]. Having just finished the fermentation schedule for the ryebock, he sat down with a few pints and added a measured amount of freshly ground peppercorn to the first, then tasted. If it was too strong, he added less to the next one. If it was too weak, he added a bit more. The process repeated until he found a good level of flavor. Once he selected the one he liked, he multiplied the weight of the pepper by 85 (as there are about 85 US pints in a firkin) and added that to the cask. He chose to use a blend of green, white, and black peppercorns. Freshly-ground peppercorns certainly have an advantage in freshness over the pre-ground pepper from the kitchen.

The takeaway here is to imagine, try, and taste.

---

[7] See Suggested Readings: Cagalione, *Extreme Brewing*

Adding Oak Character

While oak is usually added to an entire batch, individual casks can be dosed with smaller quantities of oak. Sometimes the brewer may wish to see what would have happened had they "turned it up to eleven", or were doing a trial batch of something they were considering oaking and wanted to establish a baseline from which they could extrapolate (just as Uncle Frank did above with his first pint of pepper-added ryebock). One could add oak chips or oak powder; extract flavors from the oak using steam or alcohol infusion; or add a commercial oak flavor. Many of these forms have different levels of toast: light, medium, house, and dark. The chart below helps show how different toasts impact the flavor contributed by the oak.

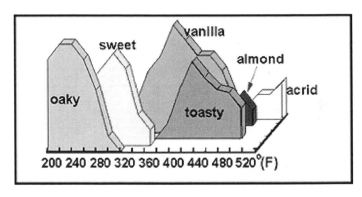

©World Cooperage, 2003

There are a couple of articles available online about oak which are mentioned in Appendix II. Regardless of how you add the oak, plan on it taking months to mellow into its full flavor.

A big disadvantage of adding oak directly to the cask is that there is no way to remove it without compromising the vessel. For brewers who maintain control over the timing, this may not be an issue. One way around this is to extract the desired flavors from the oak, then add the desired flavor directly to the cask. Steam

39

distillation of the oak works quickly but may not capture the flavors that only come out over time. Soaking the oak in a spirit such as vodka or whisk(e)y over a longer period of time can replicate the experience of the beer sitting on oak as the alcohol will penetrate more deeply into the oak. Keep in mind that the more booze you are adding, the higher the sudden change of alcohol level perceived by your yeast. Too much and the yeast may decide not to do the carbonating work for you. This is probably more relevant for a high-alcohol stout or barleywine that is already near the yeast's alcohol tolerance. In this case, consider adding a more alcohol tolerant yeast such as Danstar's Cask and Bottle Conditioning yeast (CBC) to do the conditioning work.

Adding Fruit and their Juices

We have already touched on this topic in the last chapter when we used sour cherry syrup as a priming agent. Fruit itself can be used to great effect. To get around the trouble of the fruity flesh muddying up the beer, consider using just the fresh juice instead. Trader Joes has a great line juices that are 100% juice with no added sugar or preservatives. They are great because they are known to be pasteurized so they won't serve as a contamination vector. Either way, be sure the beer has completely finished and plan on conditioning slowly in a controlled temperature environment. There is a lot of sugar in fruit and its juices and that can make for an explosive combination. As mentioned previously, consult Nutrition Facts and Information to get average sugar content of raw fruit or juices.

Someone who has lots of experience modifying cask in this way is John Geraci, head brewer at the Amherst Brewing Company in Amherst, MA. I had the opportunity to talk with him about his in-house cask program in the spring of 2015. His general advice for adding fruit directly to a cask is to get the freshest, ripest, best tasting fruit you can find then muddle it to release some of the juice. Add the whole concoction (rind, pith, everything) right to the cask before racking the beer on top of it. Store the beer in the cooler to get some measure of control over the rate it carbonates and serve just before the shive is about to pop. He has a detailed notebook on the various fruits, quantities he's added in the past, conditioning times and temperatures, and the final result that he consults when making decisions on how much to add. John doesn't worry about specific sugar contributions of the various fruits nor does he fuss about clarity when he knows it's the pulp of the fruit clouding the beer. Try it, take notes, refine your process.

Conflating Beverages

Another tack John takes is using unique flavor additions to accentuate his beer. He regularly takes inspiration from the menu at the brewpub. Oyster-accentuated stouts are only the beginning. He tells me that one of his most popular cask creations is a Bloody Mary cask. Finding the right balance of horseradish, clamato, and salt is crucial. But, when done correctly, it becomes a legend that the locals are always asking about.

The Germans have a tradition of a beer-lemonade hybrid that is a refreshing tonic after a day's cycling. They call it a radler, which is the direct translation of "cyclist" in a particular Bavarian dialect. While it is usually served as a mix of beer and sparkling lemonade, the acidity of the lemonade combined with a lower alcohol beer can create an interesting Berliner Weisse-esque brew.

There have been certain breweries that mix kombucha with beer. That they exist is all this author has to say on the topic.

Coffee has been mentioned as a possible addition. Espresso also works and contributes a much stronger flavor per unit volume.

Tea character can be introduced or reinforced. Whatever the beverage, consider using the finished liquid product instead of the source. Since the beer will be in contact with whatever has been added for an unknown time period, it is better to know how much flavor you are adding.

Whatever the mix you are adding to your cask, take notes and reflect on the results. Use these results to inform your future additions. Remember to consider the timing as a factor in what you are adding. With patience and practice, you can create excellent and novel cask ale.

CHAPTER FOUR

Serving Cask Ale

Cellar Temperature

It is important that cask ale be served at cellar temperature: 48 – 54°F (9-12°C). Proper cellar temperature maintains the appropriate levels of dissolved CO_2. As we saw in Table 2.1 from Chapter 2 (page 14), cellar temperature allows for the beer to naturally hold on to 1.1 to 1.2 dissolved volumes of CO_2. As the beer approaches room temperature, it loses the ability to hold on to appropriate levels of CO_2.

While most bars or event spaces lack an actual cellar to store casks in, other strategies can be adopted to keep the beer at the proper temperature. These will be discussed in the various service situations that follow.

Maintaining CO_2 levels has an important effect on the flavor of the beer. Without the higher carbonation levels found in kegged beer, the hop aromas of the beer are not lifted to the nose as readily. This is not to say that cask ale is doomed to have low hop character, just that relying on the CO_2 to lift the aromas is a poor strategy. There is also reduced tingling sensation on the palate. If served above cellar temperature, the beer will quickly lose all dissolved CO_2, to the detriment of flavor. *Warm and flat is not an acceptable way to serve cask ale.*

As mentioned previously, beer served ice cold actually numbs the tongue, muting the flavors of the beer. Serving at cellar temperature allows for more of the flavors in the beer to be tasted. The reduced CO_2 level, as noted above, reduces the carbonic acid component, making cask ale taste slightly sweeter than its kegged counterpart. This places an emphasis on the malt character of beer.

Brewers of cask ale recognize the impacts of service conditions and can brew their beer to take advantage of them. In England, the task of bringing out the best of what they brew is delegated to the cellarmen. There is no tradition of trained cellarmen in America. Hopefully this text along with Patrick O'Neill's excellent *Cellarmanship*[8] will help fill this gap.

Venting and Tapping

With the cask loaded onto a stillage and resting at cellar temperature, it is now time to vent and tap the cask. The basic idea is really simple - you are creating a hole in the top to vent excess condition, then punching in a tap for service later. The tools themselves are also simple.

Tools of the Trade for Venting and Tapping Casks

Woody Bits

Hard Spiles
Useful in venting and sealing the vessel. Use the wooden ones, not the plastic ones.

---

[8] See Suggested Readings: O'Neill, Patrick. *Cellarmanship*

Soft Spiles
Porous to allow excess condition to pass through. Occasionally used as a coarse air filter while drawing beer.

Useful Hand Tools

Venting Tool
This is the tool for the faint of heart that won't vent with a hard spile. Very useful with overcarbonated casks.

Gravity Tap AKA The Filton Direct Dispense Tap
This is THE tap for serving ales horizontally. Simple design, durable construction.

Straight Tap
Typically used with beer engines, these Straight Taps work for gravity service with and without a turn-down elbow.

Split or T-Tap
These uncommon taps allow for two engines to draw from the same cask. Also useful for the cellarman to monitor beer in service.

CaskWidge
This is a modern update to the old vertical extractors for serving beer on end with a beer engine.

Vertical Extractor
An older setup for serving beer on end with a beer engine. Relies on friction to hold the drawing end off of bottom. The stubby extractor body doesn't always puncture the keystone.

A venting tool is a simple way to control the release of the trapped gas within the cask. Whenever possible, allow the cask to sit on the stillage before venting. This allows time for condition released into the headspace to be reabsorbed. It also allows for acclimation to the temperature of its service environment, preferably cellar temperature. Be sure to sanitize the shive and the venting tool. Check that the valve on the venting tool is in the closed position. Hold the venting tool over the shive and knock it in with a sharp rap. Then, with the tubing safely directing possible exhaust into a container, slowly open the valve and vent the gas and foam from the vessel. If it is highly over-carbonated or infected, CO_2 can migrate out of solution and keep venting out the venting tool for an extended period of time.

A cask can be vented using only a hard spile. It has a potential to make an impressive visual display if there is significant condition to vent. Sanitize the shive then knock the hard spile in with a sharp rap. Rock the hard spile gently back and forth to work it back out and listen to the venting gas. When the pitch of the escaping gas falls, resume working the spile out until it can be removed in its entirety. If there is still a lot of foam rising, a soft spile can keep it in while venting the excess carbonation. You are far more likely to make a mess using this method so be careful.

When serving beer on end, the excess condition is vented through the tap. Once the tap has been knocked into position (see tapping, below), gas is vented out of the side of the tap similar to the venting tool, above.

Tapping is perhaps the most fun one can have with beer. The principle is really simple: drive the tap through the keystone. There is some question as to whether or not to have the spile in when venting. Leaving the spile in preserves what condition is in the beer. It also traps what condition might get knocked out of solution, causing a spike in pressure within the cask. This could cause a catastrophic failure of the spile, making for an exciting beer fountain. Taking the spile out and knocking the tap in could cause the same condition to be knocked out of solution, where it is lost. There is therefore a danger of causing the beer to be underconditioned before it even has a chance to be tasted.

I recommend *burping* the cask by removing the hard spile to vent the gas in the headspace. Replace the hard spile firmly before tapping. Once the tap is driven in, the carbonation knocked out of solution is given a chance to return before the hard spile is removed for service.

Clarity

Because cask ale is unfiltered it will inevitably contain some yeast in solution. Brewers may also add dry hops or other spices directly to the vessel. There may also be brewing artifacts such as protein clumps in the mix. None of these are attractive in the poured pint. This section will mention a few strategies to reduce or eliminate these common causes of *cloudy beer*. There will be further discussion on these strategies in the appropriate circumstance of their use later in this text.

The goal of every cellarman should be to serve the beer in the best possible condition. For this cellarman, that includes taking reasonable steps to make the beer as *bright* (brilliantly transparent) as possible. Eliminating discrete bits is an obvious first step in this process. Reducing or eliminating yeast in suspension is the next. While certain styles and breweries rely on the suspended yeast as part of their flavor profile, the vast majority do not, as evidenced by the filtering of their bottled beers. It is left to the cellarman to present the beer in the best possible light not only to make the brewery look good, but to reflect the standards of the house and encourage repeat business by building a reputation of excellent cask ale.

Bright beer begins at the brewery. The brewer must do a good job of complete starch conversion in the mash and have adequate hot and cold breaks for protein removal to have any chance of bright beer. Some styles such as wheat or wit beers will never be bright. The recent trend of extremely hoppy beers has introduced the challenge of hop protein haze. Keeping the yeast healthy throughout fermentation is also important. Filling the casks using good sanitary practices is vital to lessen the possibility of introducing contaminants such as wild yeasts or bacteria. In the UK it is common for the brewer to add a *fining agent* such as *isinglass* to the beer to help settle the yeast. A more recent trend has been to add *Alginex* (a polysaccharide-based auxiliary fining) in conjunction with isinglass.

Isinglass offends some people as it is derived from the swim bladders of certain fish. Recently a purified colloidal solution of silicic acid (SiO_2) called *BioFine Clear* (CL) has been introduced to the market. It acts in much the same way as isinglass and is slowly starting to replace isinglass in the industry.

The cellarman can act prophylactically when preparing beer for service by dosing it with finings before it is loaded on the stillage. They can be reactive and work with the beer on the stillage. Coarse physical filters can be used to hold back floaty bits. There are a variety of other strategies to encourage beer to drop bright that will be discussed later in this text.

Flavor Evaluation

The cellarman is the last link in a chain of beer production that starts with the farmer. While he or she has no control over the quality of the beer in the cask, an inattentive cellarman can turn the best beer in the world into a cloudy swill unworthy of supping. Tasting the beer before service is a critical step in serving quality cask ale. The presence of live yeast allows the flavor to evolve once the beer is stillaged, vented, and tapped. It is this evolution due to the living yeast that makes cask ale such a different product from its kegged counterparts.

Flavor evaluation is quite different from deciding if one likes a beer. The brewer makes the beer and the best guess as to their intention (from their description and/or prior personal experience with that beer) must be taken into account. The cellarman, in trying to serve the best beer possible, is looking for specific developments as the flavor evolves. Here are a few easily identifiable off flavors:

Acetaldehyde is a green apple flavor. It is an indicator the the beer is 'green', freshly tapped and young. It is typically reabsorbed by the yeast in a day or so once the carbonic acid levels are reduced by venting. High levels of acetaldehyde could be the result of too-high storage temperatures.

Thin or ***sharp mouthfeel*** is an indication of excessive carbonic acid. These levels are typically reduced by venting. The flavor should fill out a little after a day or so, especially if the carbonation levels warrant the use of a soft spile.

Vinegar or *salad dressing* flavors are a very bad sign. They usually indicate infection by a spoilage organism. Waiting a day will confirm this suspicion as it only gets worse. This is not to be confused with deliberately soured beer.

Sour flavors may be appropriate for the style. Americans have seen a rise in just about anything in casks. As someone who is not a fan of sour beer, the author was pleasantly surprised by how nice a berlinerweiss could be on cask. Besides the obvious sours, other styles such as old ale or barleywine could have this as part of their flavor profile.

Diacetyl is a very familiar flavor compound associated with buttered movie theatre popcorn. While pleasant in small doses, it is usually the fermentation byproduct of unhappy yeast. Fortunately it is quite volatile and can evaporate through the spile hole if left open. If it intensifies, this indicates an active fermentation or a contaminant working the beer.

Sulphur can come from a variety of sources. Some waters, typically in Wales, are naturally high in sulphur and inadequate venting of the boil can intensify them. Allowing the beer to age a bit on the stillage seems to reduce the perception via oxidation or palette acclimation.

DMS (*dimethyl sulfide*) is a vegetal / creamed corn flavor. It is typically produced by the yeast from a precursor compound (SMM, S-Methyl Methionine) naturally found in malt and typically removed by a vigorous boil. There's not much one can do except remove the beer from service if you determine it to be too detrimental to the flavor of the beer.

Oxidation is a wet paper or cardboard flavor. While this is typically a fault in a bottled beer, in a cask ale it is an interesting flavor contributor to be monitored. Because the cask is open to atmospheric oxygen, there will inevitably be some flavor oxidation. This isn't necessarily a bad thing. The effects are somewhat mitigated by the geometry of the vessel and the logistics of service. While beer flows from the bottom of the cask, atmosphere is pulled in at the top, albeit gently. Inside the cask there isn't much motion, so any mixing of gasses is by diffusion. There is still carbon dioxide coming out of solution, reducing contact at the surface of the beer. Even if oxygen gets to that liquid surface, there isn't much motion to encourage mixing within the liquid portion of the cask either. While the very top layer may oxidize quickly, the main body does so much more slowly. Even when it does, the living yeast interact with the dissolved oxygen and the oxidized compounds. Suffice it to say, there is a lot going on. It is this slow oxidation that contributes to the flavor evolution causing most beer to peak in flavor on the second or third day of service.

To be clear, too much oxidation is a very bad thing. A bitter or an IPA probably won't last much beyond its peak flavor as it declines pretty quickly once it reaches that peak. On the other hand, some beer, such as a wee heavy or barleywine, may be able to stand up to the oxidation for quite a long time. If the beer tastes old, stale, or tired, it's time to remove it from service.

Tasting the beer is a process of decision-making. The descriptions above are just to inform the cellarman in that process. Beer that is bad should never be served. This may mean pulling a vessel from service when there is half or more of the cask remaining. Additional tools such as a microscope might give confirmation of contamination or prove that yeast is the source of a haze. Taste the beer and make the decision.

CHAPTER FIVE

A Simple Gravity Setup using an Ice Blanket

A good friend of mine celebrates her birthday every fall with a gathering of friends. As a nod to her Germanic roots, she styles the party after Oktoberfest, the massive beer festival held annually in Munich. She made this her Oktoberfest homebrew party by asking her homebrewing friends to bring a little something to share. To separate myself from the crowd I decided a few years back to give my beer a cask presentation. This event typifies the simplest cask setup – gravity service with an *ice blanket* & cover.

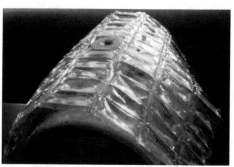 

I brew my contribution about a month ahead of the party, give it two weeks to ferment, then rack it into a *Cornelius keg* to condition. In Chapter 2 we saw the calculation for how much dextrose was necessary to prime a pin (**Example 1, Merkin's Best Bitter**) but for reasons about to become obvious, I shoot for 1.5 dissolved volumes instead of the typical 1.4.

I am filling a keg (5 gallons) with beer fermented at 70°F. According to the Table 2.2 (page 15), I can get the .69 dissolved volumes of CO_2 by using a little more than 2 ounces of dextrose. Let's use 2.1 oz to ensure that we get where we want to go.

The keg is where I am carbonating the beer and has been slightly modified for this purpose. I have installed a racking cane tip on the end of the liquid dip tube to minimize sediment that can be sucked up. CO_2 gas is only used to set the seal on the keg right after filling it with beer and again to push the finished, carbonated beer into the pin. This technique saves the bother of preparing an additional pin to serve as the conditioning vessel, then racking the carbonated beer into a second, service pin through a gravity tap. While this may disqualify it from "authentic" cask beer, since the carbonation comes from the yeast and the beer is unfiltered, I am not troubled calling it cask.

Re-racking the (hopefully) bright beer right before service is a technique called *rack bright*. It eliminates the concern about serving hazy beer due to disturbing the yeast sediment right before service by eliminating the yeast. As an extra precaution I add 10 mL of Biofine CL to the pin as I fill it. It will be well mixed in just by transporting the pin to site. It also has the benefit of being extremely fast-acting, settling out in the few hours between placing the pin in the cradle and tapping to serve. Also, I do myself a favor and cold-crash the keg the night before. This not only encourages the yeast to settle but chills the beer. Racking occurs right before transporting the beer to site on the morning of the party. The extra .1 volume of CO_2 added at the priming sugar calculation was to ensure that the carbonation lost due to racking would not leave the beer flat.

Tools of the Trade for LinzToberfest

Pin Cradle
See Chapter 11 for a technical drawing.
Made of wood, this easily holds a pin without allowing movement.

Ice Blanket
See Chapter 11 for a technical drawing.
Lays over covered pins and firkins to help keep them cool.

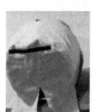

Cover
Specifically cut covers are great but a blanket or a couple of bathroom/beach towels work as well.

I usually arrive on site a few hours before the afternoon event to set up my beer and also be a help in general. For the beer I set up a table in a location where it is unlikely to be disturbed and assemble the pin cradle. The pin gets placed in it and immediately covered with the ice blanket and the cover, which is an old army-issue wool blanket that I prefer. After helping out on other tasks for an hour or so, I return and vent the pin using a hard spile. The beer shouldn't be too lively as I had worked with it just that morning. After the headspace has been vented, the hard spile is left in. The beer is now resting and settling until the start of the party.

The beer is starting out below cellar temperature and is in contact with the ice blanket. Insulating it is usually enough to keep the beer at an acceptable temperature for the afternoon and into the evening. It helps that these tend to be chilly fall nights. If her birthday was a month earlier, I might decide to take greater steps to ensure the proper serving temperature.

If you don't have an ice blanket, you could substitute a plastic bag filled with ice. Try to arrange it so that the bag does not cover the hole in the shive. A soft spile is useful here to help ensure that the hole is not blocked. You could also try the evaporative cooling method of soaking a towel in cold water and laying it over the top of the cask. As the water evaporates it pulls a little heat out of the cask. A slight wind increases the rate of evaporation, encouraging further cooling.

Linzy gets a kick out of pounding in the tap so it is her privilege to do so. Burp the headspace by removing and re-inserting the spile. Have someone hold the back of the pin in place and absorb the recoil while the tap is pounded in. I don't worry too much about sanitation in this instance as it is only in service for a few hours. Still, I do spray down the tap with StarSan. Once set, pull a half pint, dump, then offer the first taste to the birthday girl. Prosit!

CHAPTER SIX

Vertical Service using Beer Engines

The Alströms of Beer Advocate have regularly and kindly invited CASC to fulfill their mission of promoting cask ale by providing a booth at the Extreme Beer Festival (EBF). Due to the time and space constraints of the festival, doing a proper stillage is not feasible. Due to the large number of people attending, counter-top pins are insufficient volume, run the risk of being hazy, and would take up too much space. The cask solution for these conditions is to serve the firkins on end (vertically) using beer engines.

The terms "CaskWidge" and "Vertical (Beer) Extractor Body" will be conflated as Widge/Extractor as they both do the same thing. They appeared previously on page 45.

Tools of the Trade at the EBF

Large Tub
A plastic bucket big enough to hold a firkin on end with some ice around.

Beer Engine
Gently pulls beer from the cask using a vacuum created by a hand pumping motion.

Useful Hand Tools

Channel-lock Pliers
A useful hand-tool for any toolkit.

Kwik-clamp
#50 fits perfectly over reinforced ½"
ID tubing.

Setup at the EBF

The EBF is like many commercial beer festivals in that brewery representatives and volunteers only get access to the space a few hours before doors open. Beer is either chilled in buckets or sent through a jockey box. Breweries provide their own gas while the venue usually provides ice.

Cask in a hurry is possible. The beer doesn't get any time to rest after venting so the choice of what to bring relies heavily on prior experience. Beer that presents with a strong acetaldehyde or takes a while to settle is not optimal. Neither are breweries that regularly overcarbonate at priming. That said, many beers are delightful immediately after tapping. Choose one of these.

The basic setup is really simple. The firkin goes in the large tub, keystone-side up, with *some* ice. Do not *fill* it with

a firkin chilling under light ice with CaskWidge installed

ice immediately as we are not looking for ice cold beer. It'll take some experience to find the right balance. If the beer is too cold, remove as much ice as possible and allow to warm. If it is too warm, add some ice.

Attach the beer engine to your service platform. This could be a folding table at waist height but higher is better. While wrenches do work to attach the beer engine, choosing the appropriate ratchet is the superior option. Many attachment screws are right next to the glass cylinder at the heart of the beer engine. It takes only a small amount of force to break them.

If not already attached, a 6′ piece of 1/2″ reinforced (and preferably insulated) tubing is attached to the beer inlet of the beer engine and secured. Make sure that it is airtight or you will have problems with foamy pours. The other end of the tubing has a nut for attachment to the Widge/Extractor.

As always, the beer is the priority. We need vent the beer but the shive is not accessible. We'll be venting through the keystone using the Widge/Extractor.

Attaching tubing to a beer engine. It can be cramped under the bar.

Scrub the keystone with some cleanser (to remove surface mold and soils), then sanitizer. Both the CaskWidge and the Vertical Extractor have a blank insert/end that gives a surface safe to hit with the deadblow hammer. My experience (particularly with the Vertical Extractors) has been that either the body will fail to completely breach the keystone due to being so short or the force of whacking it in will cause the blank to freeze to the body. Forcibly removing it can cause breakage.

The NERAX Cellaring Crew has developed a technique using a decommissioned (read: leaky) gravity tap. They are designed to be hit and they easily breach the keystone every time. We simply attach a piece of 1/2″ tubing over the spout of the tap, then whack it in. Slowly opening the tap allows for some measure of control over headspace venting and the tubing directs any foam to a convenient receptacle. Once the beer has settled, the gravity tap is removed and the Widge/Extractor body is gently seated with a few light raps. We are putting this beer into service immediately but it could be left vented and tapped in this manner for a number of days with no detrimental effect.

Serge pulls some sanitizer through the beer engine.

With the beer vented and tapped, we just need to prepare the beer engine. This is done by pulling through some cleanser and sanitizer as time allows. At the very least, a hot rinse must be done to dislodge any dried residue from the last use. Of course this is just preventative as beer engines should be thoroughly cleaned and sanitized before storage.

Pulling through is as easy as sticking the free end of the tubing attached to the beer engine into a bucket filled with the appropriate liquid. Sharp, strong pulls are typically required to encourage liquid into a dry engine. Once there is some liquid in there to moisten the seals, the steady, measured pulls of regular service should be used.

Sometimes the engine will operate but just refuse to pull any liquid. Using a bit of tubing to force water back in through the spout is usually enough to get it working. Another way to introduce water to the cylinder is to use a large turkey baster to shoot water up the spout and into the cylinder.

Once the engine is pulling smoothly, attach the Widge/Extractor to the tubing and pull through. For the CaskWidge, this is the insert with the tubing and float attached. For the Vertical Extractor, this is the metal extractor piece. In both cases, the body of the Widge/Extractor remains sealed and seated in the keystone of the cask.

When the beer engine is ready and the festival about to begin, pull through whatever liquid may be in the line so that it is empty. Remove the blank from the body and insert the Widge/Extractor. If using a Vertical Extractor, you will have to set the Extractor height manually and secure with the nut and friction ring. Open the valve on the side of the body to allow air in as beer is removed. Pull through two pints or so and discard. Pull another half and evaluate.

If it is good, good! If it is hazy and you're using the Extractor, try raising it a bit. There isn't any time to allow for flavor development so hopefully it is a good representation of the beer. If it is significantly off, you'll have to make the decision whether or not to serve it. Putting a bad beer in front of customers in the name of using the beer is doing a disservice to the brewery, their brand, and cask itself by creating a bad impression. If necessary, obscure the name of the brewery and give it away as an example of bad cask. This is an educational booth, after all! Spoiled cask happens on occasion. However, there is no reason to throw the brewery under the bus.

There is only one real thing to troubleshoot when serving with beer engines: excessive foam in the glass. Here's a list of common causes and possible solutions:

- The line is not air-tight and is pulling air in somewhere. Check the connections at the Widge/Extractor and at bottom of engine. Usually it's the one on the bottom of the engine.

- The beer is over-conditioned. It is degassing in the cylinder. Close the side valve on the Widge/Extractor body. As additional beer is pulled, the head pressure in the firkin is reduced (increasing volume for set gas concentration). This pulls additional CO_2 out of solution to help equalize it. Eventually the keg will become locked and the handle really hard to pull. Open the valve slowly to release the vacuum. Try the beer. Be careful that you don't remove too much condition!

- Internal seal leakage. Not much you can do unless you have a seal replacement kit and know how to use it. This one just has to be dealt with for the duration of the event.

Managing the Cask While Serving

Maintaining a setup like this is simple. Periodically check the temperature of the poured beer. If it is too warm, add some ice. Too cold, remove some. The rest of the game is just chasing down the clear beer. The CaskWidge does this automatically by drawing from an inch or so below the surface of the beer. The Vertical Extractor will have to be manually repositioned a few times. Try to reposition it just above the haze demarcation line. This is a guess. If it is hazy, raise the Extractor. If bright, serve!

Pouring from a beer engine requires a bit of technique. As mentioned before, steady, measured pulls yield the best results. Hold the glass at 45° about half an inch below the spout. Pull until about half of the volume to be dispensed is in the glass. Right the glass and direct the stream of beer into the center of the glass to encourage a slight head to rise. Return the pump to its full and upright position before serving.

Swan's neck for a beer engine.

Many beer engines have a swan's neck with threading on them for a *sparkler*. This allows the beer to be delivered directly to the bottom of the glass. Popular in the north of England, this serving method is known for raising a thin, tight head on even the most stubborn of beers. Because the spout is submerged in the beer, a fresh glass is required every time a beer is poured. To do otherwise is to pose a significant health risk to the consumer. In general, they are not useful in the festival setting.

At the End of the Night

Breaking down at the end of the night is also easy. If the beer is going into service the following day, just close the vent on the body and fill with ice. The colder temperature will slow down oxidation for a bit while the closed vent prevents loss of condition. The following day requires just re-icing, opening the vent, and pulling through a pint to freshen the line.

When packing things up, plan on cleaning and sanitizing the Widge/Extractor along with the beer engine. Be sure that you drain as much sanitizer as possible out of the beer engine before storage! Shaking at various odd angles helps.

The Widge/Extractor body should also be dunked in the cleanser and sanitizer. If possible, leave these and any other sanitized bits out to air-dry before long-term storage.

The beer remaining in the firkin is best drained, then the keystone bunged for storage. TOBI your cooperage.

Tuck the firkin under the bar to maintain a clean and safe service area.

C H A P T E R   S E V E N

Blanketed Service

Casktoberfest was a private homebrew festival featuring both gravity service and beer engines. At its peak, there were two pins and six engines plus a variety of bottles. To simplify future events the host has decided to eliminate the engines in favor of a more permanent draft setup. I still serve some cask on gravity using the LinzToberfest model (Chapter 5).

This festival had the advantage of being installed in a private garage/workshop in October, which meant that the uninsulated space naturally maintained cellar temperature. The pins and kegs were brought in early in the week leading up to the event and had

Four engines and two pins in a garage

plenty of time to settle in position. The pins in their cradles were allowed to sit a day or so before venting. The kegs were also vented although this was simply opening the pressure relief valve and allowing the head pressure out. Typically the kegs had to be vented several times in the days leading up to the event as they do not breathe as the pins could.

When serving from a beer engine, any keg can do the job of holding the conditioned beer. Cornelius kegs are the easiest because they can be completely opened up for cleaning out the yeast slurry but any keg would work. The timing of this festival allows for the kegs to also serve as the conditioning vessels just as a pin or firkin could. The same calculations apply for the desired dissolved volumes of CO_2.

After the first year we used beer engines we discovered that it was advantageous to cover the beer with CO_2 instead of allowing atmosphere in. We simply didn't drink all of the beer and there was significant waste. The kegs worked great for this purpose as they are designed to accept CO_2. The only 'trick' was to set the regulator on the CO_2 supply to zero. While some may inevitably bleed past, the actual addition spread over all of the kegs (each of which already had CO_2 in solution) was sure to be negligible. For our purposes, we used a single CO_2 tank and a manifold to connect all of the

---

CO_2 or Beer Gas Mix?

Pure CO_2 is preferred over a beer gas mix or pure N_2 as partial pressure of the non-CO_2 gas would inevitably result in the beer giving up more condition than desired due to diffusion pressures. Over the time scale of this event this would be negligible but we were looking to preserve the extra beer for home consumption. In an actual cellar setting, cask ale does slowly lose its condition for just this reason. Atmospheric mix is 78% N2, 21% O2 and .04% CO2 with a host of trace gasses. Temperature and vessel configuration (constriction point at shive reduces constant mixing with air) do help preserve condition but flat beer is inevitable.

gas-sides together. A *cask breather* could have been used to ensure that excess condition could escape while ensuring that only the CO_2 necessary was allowed in to the kegs.

Connecting the beer engines to the kegs required ¼" MFL ball-lock connectors with ½" FFL swivel barbs. The beer engines have a ½" barb input. Reinforced tubing is necessary so that the vacuum created does not collapse the tube. We didn't need to insulate because of the

A Cornelius keg liquid-side connector with a 3/8" barb

configuration (kegs and tubing were under cover, venue maintained proper temperature) but doing so is easy with pipe insulation and duct tape.

Before pulling beer through the line, be sure to pull (warm) cleanser through, (warm) rinse, then cold sanitize. I prefer an iodine-based sanitizer mixed to no-rinse strength (3 mL / gallon). I like to pull the cleanser through until it is clear, then cycle it back into the source bucket for 8-12 pulls and let it sit in the line for 10-15 minutes. Agitating the cleanser inside the engine is its own reward. You'll have to hang the open end over the handle as liquids will just siphon out if left low. After sitting, pull though to empty, then pull rinse water. 8-12 pulls is fine. Do not re-cycle. Pull through, then cycle the sanitizer for 5-6 pulls. Leave packed until you're ready to connect up the lines. Pull through before connecting so that you can't possibly mix beer and sanitizer! Once connected, pull through until you get a solid stream, then take another pint (2-3 pulls). There is plenty of beer and it is not worth the hassle of worrying about early yeast sediment or tasting sanitizer residue. Just pull it through and dump it.

Attendees got a kick out of pulling their own pints. There is only one real thing to troubleshoot with engines: excessive foam in the glass. These are the same steps seen last chapter on page 61.

At the conclusion of the event, the very least that has to be done is to disconnect the gas and liquid sides of all of the kegs. To prepare the beer engines for storage, you'll need to pull through cleanser & sanitizer as before (sanitization before storage prevents mold growth due to moisture). Tilt and shake the engine every which way to remove as much sanitizer from the piston as possible.

CHAPTER EIGHT

The May Day Cask Festival

The inaugural May Day Cask Festival (MDCF) was held 10 May 2013 to celebrate the pending birth of my daughter Gianna. It was a real surprise when she showed up a month early and attended! This setup was designed to fit the space allotted to Boston's Wort Processors at the 2013 National Homebrewer's Conference Club Night in Philadelphia. I designed the setup to serve to serve five pins, three firkins, and two kegs, a total of 68 gallons of homebrew, within the time allotted for setup, service, and teardown. The MDCF was to be the proof of concept before the club took the plunge. Success!

Similar to Casktoberfest, there was a blend of gravity and engine service. The main difference was the very brief window of time available to assemble, serve, and break down the entire setup. All of the beer was racked bright in the days before delivery to the AHA Beer Cellaring Team, which stored it in a cooler. It was delivered to the site cold, which helped immensely. The problem was that even a really large room is likely to get warm when you pack such a large number of people into it. This setup needed its own cooling rig. The design was modeled after the one used at NERAX (the New England Real Ale eXhibition). It is a modular system consisting of a chilled coolant reservoir, a pump, a manifold for the colder, pump-side supply, cooling saddles, and another manifold for the warmer return-side that returned the coolant to the reservoir.

Preparing the Beer Off-Site

For both the 2013 NHC setup and the MDCF, there was not enough time in the venue to properly cellar the beer. To mitigate this fact, certain strategies were pursued to prepare the beer as well as possible off-site. This included stillaging the beer several days in advance and venting them two days before the event. This allowed time for the excess condition to be vented and the beer allowed to start the settling process. If the beer is under or properly conditioned, the additional venting time will have no negative effect as the hard spile will prevent the condition from escaping. If, as was the case for two of the beers in 2015, there is much excess condition, this can safely vent it without causing a mess at the facility.

Some of the beer was delivered in Cornelius-style kegs. The brewers assured me that they were naturally conditioned with sugar and yeast and not force-carbonated. These vessels were allowed to sit for a day in position, then vented through the pressure relief valve just like the casks. The morning of the MDCF, they were racked to service pins using a six foot length of 3/16″ tubing connected to a liquid-side ball-lock connector with a CO_2 tank and regulator gently pushing the beer from the keg into the pin at 4-5 PSI. Much like starting a siphon, the sanitizer-filled tubing was allowed to drain into a waste receptacle until it was flowing bright beer. While this may have resulted in a bit of beer waste, the lack of trub made handling the beer less worrisome. I filled the pins on end and added 10 mL of BioFine CL before sealing them with a keystone.

The beer that was already in pins I did not rack bright. Because I could set up the stillage 8 hours before the festival, I was confident that whatever trub I disturbed would have a chance to settle back down. I knew that I could move the pins without shaking them up too badly, since the venue was nearby. To help ensure settling, I added 10 mL of BioFine CL to each vessel through the spile hole before firmly seating the hard spile for transport. The gentle motion of transport mixed the finings into solution and allowed them to work more effectively.

Once on site, each pin was placed into a cradle and allowed to rest. They were not vented again until just before the festival when they were tapped. This allowed the CO_2 that was knocked out of solution a chance to go back into solution before the cask was breached again. The cooling of the casks in place assisted with this reabsorption of the CO_2 and the settling of the trub.

The Recirculating Cooling Manifold Setup

The heart of the cooling rig is a bucket of ice water. NERAX has very nice electric coolers that recirculate a glycol-water mix to do the job. Those were prohibitively expensive for an infrequent event such as the MDCF. Ice water runs pretty close to 32°F and creates a cellar-like micro-climate around each cask. Ice has the advantage of being readily available at pretty much any venue at a reasonable cost. It would be challenging to maintain over a several day festival but this service situation is only for hours. It could be done; one would simply have to remove the excess water generated by the melting ice at certain intervals.

Cooler containing ice and pump for cold water recirculation

We did require electricity as a pond pump was used to circulate the icy cold water through the manifold. The pump I use is the PondMaster Mag Drive 3. I keep the foam filter head attached to prevent ice from clogging up the intake. For the 2013 NHC stillage setup there was a proposal for a bicycle-powered pump which we thankfully did not need to follow through with. The pump is really simple to use as you submerge it and plug it in. The biggest consideration I had when making the purchase decision was the ability to lift water six feet while maintaining a decent flow rate. At three feet, the Model 3 pumps 350 gallons per hour, which seems to be sufficient for my needs.

Once chilled and pumped, the water flowed through the 'supply' side, which distributes the cold water under pressure to the various casks. My stillage was to be a collapsable six foot table, so my total length was six feet with the pins evenly spaced throughout. The NERAX version on which this was based uses an eight foot scaffolding set and fits five firkins. The main trunk is 1/2″ reinforced tubing so that it couldn't twist or collapse, restricting flow, and was convenient as the largest diameter available for the CPC Polysulfone disconnects used. The connecting distribution arms are 3/8″ diameter which worked for the quick connects used there. It also encouraged even pressure distribution in the main line, as flow resistance is greater in the smaller diameter lines. An earlier version of the NERAX manifold system relied on the John Guest push-in fittings popular at CAMRA festivals in the UK. The current iteration using the quick connects is significantly more watertight. The main points of failure are the o-rings on the male connections at the saddle.

Rear view of stillage with manifolds, quick connects, and copper saddles.

Saddles are typically constructed of stainless steel. This makes them decent conductors of heat, reasonably rigid, and inert. They are also really expensive. As of this writing, I am investigating methods for constructing them domestically. Copper is much easier to work with, provided care is taken not to pinch the tubing at any point. The saddles pictured were built by Jim Bowser by creating a jig and using a tube bending tool. Copper is slightly better at conducting heat but is so malleable that they suffer in storage. It is not uncommon to discover one kinked or split for no discernible reason. Regardless of tubing construction, compression fittings to standardize to 3/8″ FPT allow for easy installation of the male quick connects.

Side view of stillage emphasizing copper saddles

Once the cooling setup was established and the pump was circulating the icy cold water, all that was left was to cover them up a bit and make them look good. My trusty old wool blanket does just the trick. The cooling would be more efficient and effective if I had used tighter-fitting covers. For these circumstances my blanket was sufficient.

The 2015 May Day Cask Festival cellar
with cellaring team Randy & Gianna!

The plans for the cooling manifold can be found in Chapter 11: Technical Diagrams.

Venting

The remaining beer for the MDCF was served vertically using a CaskWidge and a beer engine. Since this topic has already been previously covered in Chapter 6, it is omitted here.

Cleanup

Unlike the other festivals, MDCF has a strict time limit to be clear of the venue. Unconsumed beer is unceremoniously dumped, then the casks TOBI'd. Taps get cleaned and rinsed. The beer engine is cleaned as well. Pack up and clear the hall for 10:30 PM.

C H A P T E R   N I N E

Cellaring NERAX

The New England Real Ale eXhibition (NERAX) is a real ale festival held bi-annually in the Boston metropolitan area. I have been privileged to be associated with these fine folks for a number of years, having started as a general volunteer, getting recruited onto the cellar team, and serving briefly on the Board of Directors before settling into the position of Head Cellarman. These festivals are the primary fundraisers for the Cask-conditioned Ale Support Campaign (CASC), a federally-recognized 501(c)4 non-profit tasked with educating beer drinkers, brewers, and publicans on the possibilities of cask ale done right. It has been at these festivals that I have had the opportunity to get the direct experience working with cask ale that has made this text possible.

There is a lot of work that goes into organizing a festival of this magnitude that serves 2,000+ people 100+ firkins (60+ for NERAX North) over a four (or three) day festival. While this would be a great topic for another book, at this time we are only going to focus on what needs to happen for the beer to be ready and in peak condition at the opening bell for every day of the festival. This is left in outline format for this edition.

1. The Cellar Plan – Your Guide to Survive the Festival

    a. Recruit Your Team

    b. Consolidate US & UK Beer Data

    c. The Stillage Worksheet

    d. Beer Labels for Sorting

2. Setup Day

    a. Siting & Building Stillage

    b. Sorting Beer

    c. Loading Stillage

    d. Cooling Build

    e. Bar Build

    f. Staging Verticals

3. Two Days to a Festival

    a. Venting

    b. Dispense Build

4. One Day to a Festival

    a. Tapping

    b. Verticals

5. Opening Day

    a. Preliminary Tasting

    b. Final Dispense Clean

    c. Signage

    d. Cellar Ready

    e. Maintenance During Service

    f. Dipping

    g. Beer Triage

6. Subsequent Days

    a. Tasting

    b. Signage

    c. Cellar Ready

    d. Maintaining during service

    e. Dipping

    f. Beer Triage

7. Breakdown Day

    a. Draining beer

    b. Cooling breakdown & storage

    c. Assignment of certain tasks

    d. Storage philosophy

CHAPTER TEN

Unsolicited Advice for Publicans

Dear Publican,

You don't know me and are very likely to lump me in with the beer sniffing crowd once you hear what I have to say. I really like what you are doing in bringing real ale to your establishment. Real ale aficionados can be some of the most persnickety but also the most loyal of your customer base. Please allow me to share some of my experience working with real ale to help you appease even the stodgiest CAMRA member.

I think that cask ale presents a very different take on the same brewery products you may already have on draught. It seems that to be successful, cask ale needs a critical mass of demand so that it can turn over quickly enough to be financially viable. Some bars do this by restricting availability to Thursday tappings (which yields peak flavor on Friday or Saturday). Wanting to provide cask regularly is tougher. I would hate for you to give a negative impression to cask ale drinkers who have a certain ideal in mind while you build the critical mass necessary for your business to prosper. As they say, once bitten, twice shy.

What makes this a little more difficult is the non-confrontational nature of today's consumer. They may not make a fuss by asking for another pour or refusing a served pint in person but they have no problem griping on Yelp or telling their friends about poor cask. Even if they keep to themselves, giving a curious drinker a poor pint of cask ale prejudices them against trying cask again in the future.

There are two primary factors that determine quality cask: temperature and time. You will get the best flavors and carbonation when the beer is at cellar temperature. At the appropriate temperature the beer will naturally hold on to the appropriate amount of CO_2 for this presentation. If the beer is allowed to rise to room temperature, it will taste too warm and will rapidly lose carbonation.

I am very concerned about the presentation of warm, flat beer as cask ale being detrimental to your future trade. Those who have experienced cask before will be put off and write you off in the future. I've definitely done this with certain establishments that I've found to be underwhelming. As a publican, you know that you need to present your best face every time to every customer to build your business. While some people may not mind or may even prefer what I would consider to be a fault[9], when enough people bias themselves with preconceptions of what cask ale could be, your presentation will be found to be lacking and you will lose their future business as repeat customers for your real ale. You can avoid this by serving cask ale at the appropriate temperature. Strategies for doing so include cask-specific refrigerators, tapping into glycol lines, building special protrusions from a walk-in cooler, or setting up a cooling loop using a cold plate in your ice well.

I am, of course, spoiled with my festival experience as I get to try beers when they have been freshly tapped and as they evolve

---

[9] Ariely, Dan, http://people.duke.edu/~dandan/Papers/PI/Beer.pdf

over the several days of our festival. The business model of a festival is decidedly different from your experience. We are under no financial pressure to sell every drop of every beer. We need only provide sufficient options for our customers to be satisfied until the closing bell. As such, we have the leisure to concern ourselves with optimal cellar temperatures, carbonation, and peak flavor.

Peak flavor has very much to do with how long the beer has been in service. Over time, oxidative effects will slowly change a green, freshly tapped beer into a beer at its peak flavor, then continue down the slope towards a progressively insipid ale. Most of the pale, hoppy beers in vogue these days will have a two to four day service life. Some of the stronger ales of winter may be able to last up to a week. The rare barleywine will hold up well into a second week. If you have insufficient trade, you must dispose of tired ale. Serving it to gain the benefit of a couple of pints sold today is not worth the loss of your future business.

Cask ale done right can draw a certain segment of the beer-drinking public. Do it right consistently and you will find a regular and dedicated drinking crowd. Thank you for considering what I had to say. I hope to have a pint with you at your fine establishment someday soon. Until then, be well.

Cheers,

-- Randy Baril
Cask Ale Enthusiast
Head Cellarman, CASC

CHAPTER ELEVEN

Technical Drawings

Here are a few diagrams that should help you duplicate the success that I have found. When specified, part numbers are from FOXX Equipment, Inc.

Pin Ice Blanket

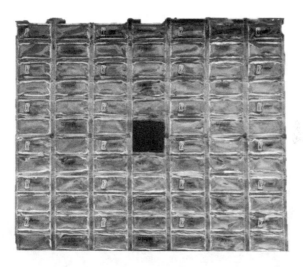

This is cut from a larger sheet of an ice blanket common in the food service industry. It measures 12 cells by 7 cells, which is about 17" x 24". The center two cells are removed to allow easy access to the shive. When frozen before use, this is a lightweight, reusable, and flexible cooling solution that does not get soggy or wet.

Pin Cradle

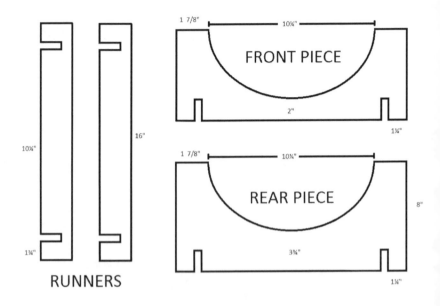

This can be made from plywood or whatever lumber is available. Finishing it can make it look very nice.

Cooling Manifold (need 2 per bay)

(1) PLC Quick Connects, Female barbed w/ shutoff (05P01-190)

(2) 5" lengths of 3/8" ID reinforced tubing (08H05-152)
       For firkins, use 9½" lengths.

(A) Oetiker stepless clamps, 17.0, 11/16" (06G08-183)

(3) Plastic Tee, ½"B x ½"B x 3/8"B (05G01-185)

(4) 18¾" lengths of ½" ID reinforced tubing (08H05-103)

(5) 8" lengths of ½" ID reinforced tubing

(B) Oetiker stepless clamps, 21.0, 13/16" (06G08-201)

(6) HFC35 Quick Connect, ½" Straight Hose Barb, Male, w/ Shutoff (05P01-152)

(7) HFB35 Quick Connect, ½"Straight Hose Barb, Female, w/ Shutoff (05P01-151)

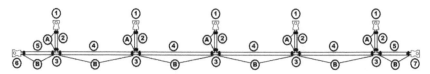

Stainless Steel Saddles for Firkins

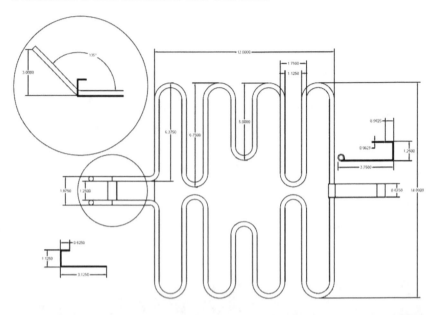

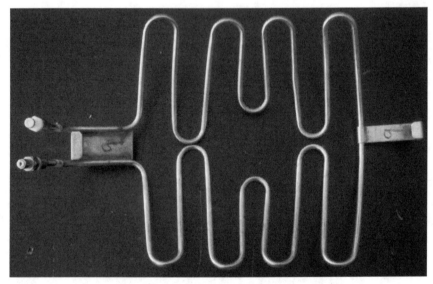

Attached to the saddle are two 5/16" OD compression by ¼" NPT female connectors to which male PLC Quick Connects (04P01-114 and 05P01-186) are attached.

Vertical Extractor

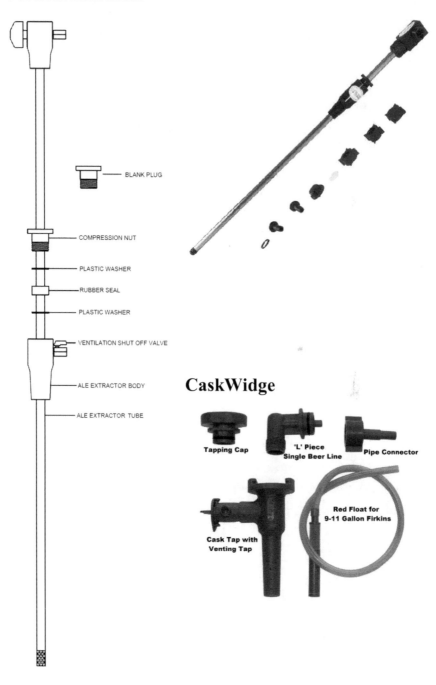

BLANK PLUG

COMPRESSION NUT

PLASTIC WASHER

RUBBER SEAL

PLASTIC WASHER

VENTILATION SHUT OFF VALVE

ALE EXTRACTOR BODY

ALE EXTRACTOR TUBE

CaskWidge

Tapping Cap

'L' Piece
Single Beer Line

Pipe Connector

Cask Tap with
Venting Tap

Red Float for
9-11 Gallon Firkins

Glossary of Terms

alpha acidity, 25 - This is the percentage by weight of the alpha acids of the hops used in brewing. Alpha acids must be boiled to taste bitter through the process of isomeration.

beer flavors[10]:

acetaldehyde, 49 - fresh cut green apples, usually from incomplete fermentation, oxidation, or bacterial infection.

acetic (vinegar or salad dressing), 50 - pungent, sharp, or tart flavors along with thinning mouthfeel commonly associated with vinegar or salad dressing. Usually indicative of infection.

diacetyl, 50 - movie theater butter or caramel butterscotch with an associated slick mouthfeel. Sometimes associated with certain yeast strains, incomplete fermentation, or infection.

DMS, dimethyl sulfide, 50 - a sweet, cooked corn or vegetable aroma and flavor. Usually a byproduct of a poor mash or weak boil while brewing. Sometimes bacterial infection.

mouthfeel, thin or sharp, 49 - beer just tastes watery.

oxidized, 50 - vinous, wet cardboard, sherry, vegetative flavors and aromas due to atmospheric oxygen.

sour, 50 - similar to acetic but more closely related to pH. Sometimes appropriate. Less salad dressing, more lemonade.

sulphur, 50 - hydrogen sulphide, that rotten egg or burning match flavor or aroma. Occasionally a characteristic of the brewing liquor. Usually a bacterial infection.

---

[10] Adapted from Janson, Lee W., *Brew Chem 101*, Chapter 5: Understanding and Avoiding Off Flavors, p57-87

bilge, 10 - the widest part (belly) of the cask.

blanketed service, 5 - replacing the gas in the headspace of a cask with CO2 as beer is poured.

bright beer, 47 - beer that is sufficiently translucent due to a lack of protein haze, yeast in suspension, or other clouding agents.

bung, 11 - a piece of cork that plugs the keystone after the tap is removed. More generally, any bit that seals a bung hole.

bung hole, 10 - the hole in the bilge of a cask where the shive goes. More generally, any hole in a vessel.

butt, 6 - half of a tun, which is two hogsheads or three barrels. It is 108 imperial gallons.Campaign for Real Ale (CAMRA), 1

carbonation, 2 - the amount of CO2 dissolved in a liquid. Usually measured in volumes of CO2.

cask ale, 5 - beer served at cellar temperature with 1.1 to 1.3 dissolved volumes of CO2. It must be served mechanically without the aid of compressed gasses to push it to the point of dispense.

CAMRA definition of, 5 - "Real ale is a natural product brewed using traditional ingredients and left to mature in the cask (container) from which it is served"

cask breather, 66 - a device that allows excess condition to vent while only allowing in CO2 to replace volumes of beer dispensed.

cask cradle, 8 - a stand that holds a cask in service position.

Cask Widge™, 45 - a device for serving cask ale vertically.

caustic, 12 - a cleaning chemical with a very high pH.

cellar temperature, 2 - 48 to 54°F (9 to 12°C)

cellarman, 6 - the person, regardless of sex, who prepares and maintains cask ale for service.

chock, 8 - a piece of wood cut as a right triangle to hold a cask secure in service position. Usually 3" x 4" x 5".

chocking, 7 - the act of placing chocks, hypotenuse down in a three point orientation that maximizes contact with the cask

cloudy beer, 47 - typically an immature ale that has significant yeast in suspension.

CO_2, 2 - carbon dioxide, either as a gas or as carbonic acid

condition, 4 - the carbonation level with respect to the other flavors present in a beer.

cooperage, 7 - an expansive term for any large vessel that holds beer.

dextrose, 16 - a molecule of glucose in linear form. $C_6H_{12}O_6$.

dry hopping, 23 - the act of adding untreated hops directly to a fermentation or serving vessel.

fermentable, 16 - any simple sugar that can be digested by yeast.

final gravity, 19 - the specific gravity reading at the end of fermentation.

finings, 48 - an agent added to a beer to encourage clarity.

Alginex, 48 - a polysaccharide-based auxiliary fining with strong negatively-charged molecules derived from algae and produced by Murphy & Son of Nottingham, UK. Must be used in conjunction with isinglass or BioFine to be effective.

BioFine Clear (CL), 48 - a purified colloidal solution of silicic acid produced by Kerry of Ireland.

isinglass, 48 - a pure, transparent or translucent form of gelatin, obtained from the air bladders of certain fish, usually the sturgeon.

firkin, 6 - a cask that holds 9 imperial gallons, which is equivalent to two pins or half of a kilderkin. This is the most common vessel in the trade.

floaty bits, 24 - small clumps of protein or hop particulate large enough to see. Can be filtered out with a scrubbie.

front end, 9 - The front face of the cask that contains the keyhole.

gravity, 2 - See *specific gravity*.

hard spile, 44 - a wooden or plastic peg that seals the shive when a cask is not in active service.

headspace, 10 - the volume within a vessel not occupied by liquid.

hogshead, 6 - a quarter tun, which is three kilderkin. It is 54 imperial gallons.

ice blanket, 52 - see technical drawing, page 81.

keg, Cornelius, 53 - a pressure-capable vessel popular with homebrewers. It has a large hatch for interior access and two ball-lock ports that separates the inlet and the outlet.

keyhole, 10 - the hole in the front end where the tap is placed, typically in conjunction with a keystone.

keystone, 10 - the wooden or plastic bung that occupies the keyhole. See page 10 for pictures.

kilderkin, 6 - half of a barrel, which is two firkins. 18 imp. gallons.

krausening, 20 - the practice of introducing un- or actively-fermenting wort to a finished beer before packaging to produce the necessary carbonation.

pin, 6 - half of a firkin, which is 4.5 imperial gallons.

proper, 1 - an colloquial term refering to the house's go-to beer. Similar to ordering a "lager" or "IPA". Could also refer to a "proper English ale", which would, of course, be cask!

rack, racked, 12, **racking**, 16 - the infinitive, past participle, and present participle of the act of moving liquids from one vessel to another.

rack bright, 53 - a technique that separates cask ale that is ready to serve from the sedimentation created by the yeast that carbonated it. While it jeopardizes the longer-term flavor developments by introducing massive amounts of oxygen, in a shorter-term serving situation it allows for the service of bright beer when there is insufficient time to properly cellar it.

rack-bright beer, 5 - beer that has been racked bright into a new serving vessel while leaving behind all sediment from the conditioning fermentation.

real ale, 4 - any beer (ale or lager, despite the name) that has undergone a secondary fermentation in a sealed vessel.

sanitizing, 12 - the process of reducing microbiological contamination to an acceptable level.

service vessel, 16 - the vessel from which finished beer is served.

shive, 10 - a bung that seals the bung hole in the bilge of a cask.

soft spile, 45 - a wooden peg made of soft, porous wood that allows gas to travel through.

sparkler, 62 - an attachment to a beer engine that raises a thin, tight head by forcing the beer through a series of small holes. To work properly, beer must be delivered to the bottom of the glass.

specific gravity, 20 - a measure of density of a liquid.

spile, 10 - a general term for a small peg, usually wood, that seals the hole in a shive. See also *hard spile, soft spile*.

spoilage organisms, 3 - any microorganism that can survive in beer and impact the flavor.

stillage, 7 - a place for casks of beer to rest in their service orientation to encourage sediment to accumulate in a convenient place where it will not be served.

tap (verb), 10 - the act of driving a tap (noun, below) into a cask.

tap (noun) - a device that controls the flow of beer out of a cask.

> **Gravity (Direct Dispense)**, 45 - a tap for serving a beer horizontally without using a beer engine.

> **Split or T-tap**, 45 - a tap that allows two beer engines access to a single cask OR allows the cellarman to test the beer in a cask without having to disconnect a beer engine line. Must be used horizontally.

> **Straight**, 45 - a tap with a single valve usually used with beer engines. Can be used for gravity service, typically with an elbow tailpiece. Must be used horizontally.

see also: *CaskWidge, vertical extractor*

TOBI, 11 - Tap Out, Bung In, an acronym to describe sealing a cask after service.

tun, 6 - two butts, which is 216 Imperial gallons.

venting, 10 - the act of releasing carbonation in the headspace

> **burping the cask**, 47 - removing the spile of a vented cask, allowing the excess carbonation out, then resealing with the spile. Typically done before tapping.

venting tool, 45 - a device for breaching the shive that allows excess condition to vent in a controlled manner.

vertical extractor, 45 - a device that allows for the service of cask while on end. Must be used with a beer engine.

volumes of CO_2, 14 - the volume that the CO_2 in gaseous form would occupy at one atmosphereic pressure and 0°F were it not dissolved in the beer.

woody bits, 10 - the shive, keystone, spiles, or bungs that are used in sealing a cask. These are single-use items.

wort, 16 - unfermented beer

A P P E N D I X   I I

Suggested Reading

Brewgeeks. "Toasted Oak Cubes", accessed March 13, 2015, http://www.brewgeeks.com/toasted-oak-cubes.html

Brew Your Own Magazine. "Carbonation Priming Chart", accessed February 24, 2015, https://byo.com/resources/carbonation

Calagione, Sam. *Extreme Brewing: An Enthusiast's Guide to Brewing Craft Beer at Home.* Crestline Books, 2012.

Fix, George. *Vienna, Märzen, Octoberfest.* Boulder: Brewers Publications, 1991

Home Distillation of Alcohol. "Charcoal & Wood Flavouring", accessed March 13, 2015, http://homedistiller.org/aging/aging/wood

Janson, Lee W.. *Brew Chem 101: The Basics of Homebrewing Chemistry.* North Adams: Story Press, 1996

Line, David. *The Big Book of Brewing.* GW Kent, 1982

Monya, Pauline, and Tonya Tokara, Peggy Panga, Alexandra Fiegela, Jean-François Meulleneta, Han-Seok Seo. "Temperature of served water can modulate sensory perception and acceptance of food" *Food Quality and Preference* 28 (2013): 449–455

Mosher, Randy. *Radical Brewing: Recipes, Tales & World-Altering Meditations in a Glass.* Boulder: Brewers Publications, 2004

Palmer, John J. *How to Brew: Everything you need to know to brew beer right the first time.* Boulder: Brewers Publications, 2006

O'Neill, Patrick. *Cellarmanship*, 6th edition. St Albans: CAMRA Books, 2016